Low-Fat Soul

Low-Fat Soul

Jonell Nash

One World

The Ballantine Publishing Group
New York

A One World Book
Published by The Ballantine Publishing Group

http://www.randomhouse.com

Grateful acknowledgment is made to the following for permission to reprint previously
published material:

DUTTON SIGNET: Recipe for "Skinless Fried Chicken" from DOWNHOME WHOLESOME by Danella
Carter. Copyright © 1995 by Danella Carter. Reprinted by permission of Dutton Signet, a
division of Penguin Books USA Inc.

TIMES BOOKS: Recipe for "Decadent Devil's Food Cake with Creamy Fudge Frosting" from
AMERICAN HEART ASSOCIATION COOKBOOK, Fifth Edition. Copyright © 1993 by American Heart
Association. Reprinted by permission of Times Books, a division of Random House, Inc.

Library of Congress Catalog Card Number: 97-97059

ISBN: 0-345-41363-6

Cover art and design by Heather Kern

Manufactured in the United States of America

First Hardcover Edition: August 1996
First Trade Paperback Edition: January 1998
10 9 8 7 6 5 4

For Tee (my aunt Alberta O. Sparks),
who, decades before the need to change our diet became evident,
was an advocate of low-fat, healthful eating.

As an early home economist, she led the way for others,
like myself, to follow.

Contents

Acknowledgments

To all who gave of their professional skills, their cherished recipes, and themselves in the creation of this book, I offer my deepest gratitude.

Special thanks to Joëlle Delbourgo for her vision in getting this project underway and to my Ballantine editor, Ginny Faber, and her assistant, Beth Bortz, and associate managing editor Cindy Berman for giving it vitality. Much appreciation to literary agent Carla Glasser for bringing all of us together.

Being surrounded by the talent and sisterhood of the ESSENCE editorial staff is one of my blessings. Heartfelt thanks to Pamela Johnson, Rosemarie Robotham, Janice Bryant, and LaVon Leak-Wilks.

Kendra London, Cerene Roberts, and Robin Taylor diligently kept the mechanics of my bookwriting moving. Amanda Cushman and Rhonda Stieglitz helped test, taste, and refine recipes. Mindy Hermann provided nutritional analysis, as well as sound suggestions for losing the fat. Mary Wirth and Kristine Mills-Noble turned a ream of manuscript pages into a visual work of art; Judd Pilossof captured the image on the cover.

My dear sisters, Gertrude Cherry and Marva Stanton, helped breathe new life into old memories.

Paul Butler lovingly saw me through it all.

And finally, my supreme admiration and thankfulness to the nameless ones who have gone before me and paved the way.

Low-Fat Soul

Introduction

Flava!

Cooking reflects the nature of its people. So it's not at all incidental that traditional African American cooking is known as "soul food." Even more than specific dishes or ingredients, soul food represents a certain spirit, an attitude, a flamboyance, a kind of loving that one brings to the kitchen and stirs into the pots. In essence, it's a flava.

Our flava reaches back across the waters to West Africa and beyond. Seeds, techniques, and taste memory traveled in our stash and in our hearts as we made the arduous journey to this country in shackles. Soul food was then born in the slave quarters of southern plantations as our ancestors pieced together amazing meals mainly from scraps and leftovers. After choice portions were selected for the "master's" table, the remaining neck bones, hock, tails, and tough cuts, along with cornmeal, molasses, lard, and other staples, were then rationed to the workers. Our ancestors supplemented their makeshift pantries with produce from their gardens, along with seafood and game caught in local waters and nearby woods. Greens, okra, sweet peppers, corn, lima beans, shrimp, crawfish, catfish, possum, rabbit, and squirrel became the makings of flavorful repasts that held together body, mind, and spirit. In those painful days of our history, a satisfying meal was one of few joys—so, much care was given to the preparation. Then, as now, our food witnessed the stories of our lives—christenings, rites of passage, anniversaries, and wakes.

Our forebears gave little thought to the fat or sugar stirred in. Besides, they burned off much of what they ate during long, grueling days toiling in the fields. Fat in the diet was actually

important to survival. Our lives have changed dramatically since then. But we still hunger for those flavors, and we still pile our plates high. And many of us, as our forebears did, stir in as much butter, lard, and fatty pan drippings as it takes to make a dish taste wonderful—filled with . . . flava. But the last two decades have shown us we must change our ways. Numerous research studies have proven that excess fat increases the risk of dying prematurely from heart disease or cancer. Living high on the hog and high-fat foods are also linked to obesity and kidney failure. The 1995 guidelines from the USDA recommend that total fat in the diet be less than 30 percent of total daily calories. This is about 65 grams of fat for a person who eats 2,000 calories a day. Easing the percentage down to 25 percent, or about 54 grams, may prove even more beneficial.

Soul food—our fabled, spirited fare—is frequently too high in fat and salt, and a link to numerous and widespread health problems in our community. Our saving grace is that many traditional African American foods are excellent sources of vital nutrients. Cabbage, greens, and other members of this cruciferous family are known as anti-cancer vegetables. Sweet potatoes are loaded with beta carotene (vitamin A), and black-eyed peas and other flavorful legumes are loaded with protein and dietary fiber. So the question becomes, how do we lose the health-harming effects and restore the power to our favorite dishes while preserving our time-honored tradition?

LOW-FAT SOUL is the answer. It offers you a fresh start, blending the old with the new, the familiar with the unexpected. It offers you a cornucopia of ideas for awakening exciting flavors with fresh herbs, hot peppers, lively spices, aromatic vegetables, and other natural seasonings and sweeteners. You'll learn to embrace cooking methods that "defat" instead of add fat to foods. Our kitchens can once again fill with heady aromas, full pots, hospitality, and love.

LOW-FAT SOUL also pays tribute and honor to the legions of outstanding black cooks who toiled with love in the creation of this world-class cuisine. In the "big house" on plantations large and small, on wagon trains and cattle drives, in railroad dining cars, in hotels and inns, and in their own homes, the largely unheralded culinary talents of our pioneering forebears marked the development of American cooking. Soul food and southern cooking are so intermingled that distinctions are not readily discernible. It is evident that many of the foods of the South—wild greens, sweet potatoes, watermelons, black-eyed peas, and okra—as well as methods of preparation and seasonings, reach back throughout the Caribbean islands and directly to Africa. The most famed of southern dishes are the Creole specialties of New Orleans. Satisfying, succulent dishes such as jambalaya, étouffée, and gumbo are among those African cooks culled from signature ingredients of the city's diverse ethnic population.

Recent years have brought us prominent chefs, writers, and restaurateurs who shine light on the range and depth of contributions African Americans have made to this country's food legacy. Edna Lewis is unquestionably the crown (perhaps toque) jewel. Jessica Harris has been especially prolific in authoring books on our culinary history and culture. Patrick Clark, as executive chef of Tavern on the Green in New York City, continues to make history. Young, credentialed torchbearers are emerging from prestigious cooking schools across the nation, guaranteeing that our history will endure, continue to evolve, and be celebrated! Today, traditional African American cooking holds a place among the fine cuisines of the world. Here in the United States, dishes such as spoonbread, stewed black-eyed peas, and fried okra appear on the menus of trendy restaurants from coast to coast. Busloads of Japanese tourists pack Sylvia's, a landmark Harlem restaurant, for a taste of smothered chicken and candied yams. And in the city known for the loftiest of culinary standards, Parisians and American expatriates pack the tiny quarter of Ray's for braised collard greens and hot biscuits.

Low-Fat Soul is a guide to contemporary African American cooking—fresh, authentic flavors with a twist. I'm excited about this new day, our expanded realm of choices that provides us with the best that life has to offer. There's personal power in making sound decisions and following through. Choose to eat more healthfully so that you may have the stamina, vitality, and longevity to reach your personal goals and fulfill your special mission. Continue to add flava in everything you do.

Cook and enjoy meals with your family and friends, so that the spiritual bonds among us will be continuously renewed and strengthened.

Savor the Flavor

Taste is tops when it comes to eating pleasure. And soul food has flavors like no other. Herbs, spices, and other natural seasonings are the keys to exciting the palate and adding substance to dishes in more health-conscious ways.

BOOT THE FAT, BOOST THE FLAVOR

PEPPERS—Once so precious they were used as money. Hot peppers (chiles) are a trademark of African and Caribbean cooking. Use peppers in their fresh, dried, ground, roasted, pickled, or smoked forms to add spunk to your pots. As a rule, bigger chiles are tamer, while small ones tend to be sharp and fiery. The Scotch bonnets of the Caribbean top the heat scale, and add flavor as well as bite.

ONIONS, GARLIC, LEEKS, SHALLOTS, AND SCALLIONS—All members of the onion family can be used in flavoring almost all savory dishes and even breads. Use more than one for depth. Dried onion and garlic products can't compete with the quality of fresh ones.

CELERY AND GREEN BELL PEPPERS—When combined with onions, they form the holy trinity of Creole cooking. These fresh ingredients add such fragrance and flavor, they should be used almost routinely.

CITRUS JUICE AND ZESTS—Use in sauces, poultry, fish, vegetables, salad dressings, and baking. The colored outer portion of peel is rightly called "zest"; grate or thinly slice, avoiding the bitter white pith.

GINGER—Fresh ginger can be sliced, chopped, julienned, or grated to add spicy, peppery, lemony undertones to fish, stir-fry dishes, and vegetables such as carrots. Ground ginger has a different nature—use it to add sweet aroma and clovelike flavor to baked goods, sweets, and beverages.

SMOKED FOODS—Smoke-cured chicken, turkey, sausages, trout, hot peppers (chipotle), and even cheese replace smoked bacon or ham in adding woody, outdoor flavor to broths, bean soups, stews, and greens.

VINEGAR—There's a world of varieties that include apple cider, wine, malt, rice, balsamic, and the newer infused vinegars made by steeping fresh herbs or fruits. Distilled white vinegar has a harsh taste and is best kept for pickling.

WINE, SPIRITS—Dry red and white wines, brandy, sherry, rum, and other spirits add instant flavor to sauces, soups, entrées, and desserts. Most of the alcohol is lost during cooking, leaving the desired twang. Avoid cooking wines; they tend to be very salty.

FROM THE HERB GARDEN AND SPICE RACK

Herbs give foods a burst of flavor and aroma without adding sodium or calories. Fresh herbs have a livelier flavor dimension than dried versions; however, dried herbs have more intensity because their flavor concentrates as the moisture is removed. Therefore, when substituting dried for fresh versions of an herb, the ratio is 1 teaspoon of dried to 3 teaspoons (1 tablespoon) fresh. Having a flair with herbs simply comes from use and a little experimenting. Most supermarkets now carry an impressive selection of fresh herbs in addition to a wide choice of dried herbs. I find these herbs and spices to be the most helpful to have on hand: allspice, basil, bay leaves, caraway, cardamom, celery seed, chili powder, chives, cinnamon, cloves, crushed red pepper, cumin, curry, dill, fennel, ginger, leeks, mint, nutmeg, oregano, paprika, parsley, rosemary, saffron, sage, tarragon, and my favorite—thyme.

Coming to Terms with Fat

The following definitions will guide you through this book, and help as you read food labels when shopping. Consider these terms "words to live by."

CHOLESTEROL and fat are not the same thing. Cholesterol is a fatlike substance synthesized by the body and present in all animal foods—meat, poultry, fish, milk and milk products, and egg yolks. Plants do not contain cholesterol. Dietary cholesterol raises blood cholesterol levels in many people, increasing their risk for heart disease.

FATS are the concentrated source of energy for the body. All forms of fat contain a combination of the following three types of fatty acids. All fats, however, are not created equal.

1. Saturated fats are naturally solid at room temperature; these fats can raise blood cholesterol levels. Lard, butter, and hydrogenated shortening are examples.
2. Monounsaturated fats are liquid at room temperature and may decrease blood cholesterol. Olive oil, canola oil, peanuts, and fish are rich in monounsaturated fats.
3. Polyunsaturated fats are liquid at room temperature. Corn, sunflower, and soybean oils are examples.

BUTTER: Churned cow's milk used as cooking fat or a spread. Eighty percent fat, more than half of which is saturated. Imparts unique, rich flavor and texture. Use sparingly.

Light or soft butter: Water replaces most of the reduced fat, resulting in a substitute with half the calories and fat of butter. Substitute equal amount for butter. When baking, decrease liquid in recipe slightly to compensate for the added water content.

MAGARINE: Developed as a butter substitute, magarine contains 100 calories per tablespoon, the same amount as butter. Major differences between the two are that butter contains cholesterol and about three times more saturated fat. Margarine is made from unsaturated vegetable oils, such as canola, corn, or sunflower, then hydrogenated to provide the consistency of butter. The process of hydrogenation forms trans-fatty acids, which behave much like artery-clogging fats. The issue of trans-fatty acids makes an across-the-board advantage of switching from butter to margarine questionable. Select margarine that contains no more than 2 grams of saturated fat per tablespoon (read the label).

Reduced-fat (tub) margarine: Contains 60 percent or less fat. Less hydrogenated than standard stick margarine, it contains fewer saturated fats and trans-fatty acids.

Low-fat (whipped) margarine: Pumping regular margarine with air makes this product very spreadable. Measure for measure, it contains about half the fat of regular stick margarine (no more than 40 percent fat).

VEGETABLE COOKING OILS: These liquid fats are the kinds of fats to rely on in your daily diet. Olive oil is highest in monounsaturated oils and is considered the most healthful. Canola and peanut oil are other monounsaturated oils. Safflower is the most polyunsaturated oil; soybean, sunflower, corn, and sesame oils follow in descending order.

VEGETABLE SHORTENING: Vegetable oils are pumped with hydrogen to make them semisolid. Shortening produces tender baked goods. Hydrogenation, unfortunately, creates trans-fatty acids, which may raise blood cholesterol levels.

NONSTICK VEGETABLE COOKING SPRAY: A thin layer of spray (keep a light touch) adds an insignificant amount of fat to food. In addition to plain, these sprays are now available in butter and olive oil flavors.

TROPICAL OILS—COCONUT OIL, PALM KERNEL OIL, AND PALM OIL: Unlike other plant oils, these oils contain a higher percentage of saturated fat than unsaturated fat. Reddish-orange palm oil lends a distinct flavor and color to many West African, Caribbean, and Brazilian dishes. Use sparingly or avoid (check package labels) to limit saturated fat.

LARD: Rendered hog fat, long a staple of cooking in the Deep South. Produces the flakiest of biscuits and pastries, but it's pure fat and much of it is saturated. One tablespoon contains 116 calories and 13 grams of fat. Avoid at all costs.

How to Use Nutritional Analysis

Each recipe in this book provides a calculation of the calories, fat, cholesterol, protein, and sodium in a serving. This informa-

tion is a fair estimate for you to use in monitoring your intake and making food choices. Nutritional analysis is not, however, an exact science; some variables cannot be controlled and other information may be overlooked or not taken into account. For example, take a chicken recipe: All chickens obviously do not contain the same amount of fat; some are bred leaner than others. There are other questions: How scrupulously was the visible fat removed before cooking? How much fat remained in the skillet? How much fat was left on the plate? So don't get caught up in a lot of counting. A well-balanced diet that features fresh foods and follows clear and obvious methods to keep fat and calories low will be healthful.

Use these guidelines to stay on track.

CALORIES—Limit calories to 1,600 for sedentary women and older adults; 2,200 for most children, teenage girls, active women, and many sedentary men (women who are pregnant or breastfeeding may require more); 2,800 for teenage boys, many active men, and some very active women. Burn up more calories than you take in, and you'll lose weight; take in more than you use, and you'll gain.

PROTEIN—The amount of protein needed daily is determined by age and body size; the general U.S. RDA for adults is 65 grams. Multiply your body weight by 0.36. For example, a 120-pound woman needs 43.2 grams. Pregnant women need about 30 grams more protein every day than nonpregnant women. Nursing mothers should add an extra 20 grams of protein to their diet every day until their children are weaned.

FAT—Limit fat to 30 percent of calories. This amounts to 53 grams of fat in a 1,600 calorie diet, 73 grams of fat in a 2,200 diet. Limit saturated fat to less than 10 percent of calories, or about one-third of total fat intake. Note: One teaspoon of fat equals about 4.4 grams of fat.

CHOLESTEROL—Limit intake to about 300 milligrams a day.

SODIUM—Keep intake between 1,100 and 3,000 milligrams per day. One teaspoon of salt contains about 2 milligrams of sodium. Most Americans consume 4,000 to 8,000 milligrams daily.

NOTE: Optional ingredients and those mentioned as "if desired" serving suggestions are not included in the analysis.

A Measurable Difference

The cooks of old fully engaged their senses. They measured by smidgens, pinches, and handfuls, and knew exactly when food was done by its color or burst of aroma. This is a talent that takes time to hone. Until you develop your own food sense, you can rely on proven recipes to avoid the disappointment and costliness of trial and error. The following recipes have all been carefully tested, and some retested, to make them near fail-proof. Because of the science involved in baking, it's best to follow those directions to the letter; correct measuring can prove crucial. Otherwise, improvise—that's our tradition. But here's how to get the best results from LOW-FAT SOUL recipes.

You need:

- Two types of measuring cups. Liquid ingredients require a clear glass or plastic cup with a spout; 1-cup and 2-cup sizes are the handiest. Dry ingredients require metal or plastic cups that have handles and come usually in a set of four sizes: ¼ cup, ⅓ cup, ½ cup, and 1 cup.
- Set of measuring spoons. These come in sets of four with the standard measurements of ¼ teaspoon, ½ teaspoon, 1 teaspoon, and 1 tablespoon.

To measure dry ingredients such as flour, cornstarch, and confectioners' sugar by the cupful, lightly spoon the ingredient in the proper size measuring cup, then sweep off the excess with the back of a knife. Do not shake the cup or pack the ingredient down (except for brown sugar, which should be lightly pressed). For smaller quantities, lightly spoon the ingredient into the appropriate size measuring spoon and sweep off the excess. This method is more consistent than dipping the cup or spoon into the ingredient and then sweeping across the top; dipping tends to pack the ingredients in varying degrees and makes results more unreliable. Measure solid ingredients such as yogurt, vegetable shortening, and nuts in dry measuring cups.

To measure liquid ingredients such as water, milk, or honey, pour the ingredient into a clear measuring cup up to the required mark. For accuracy, check the level of the ingredient by bending down to view it at eye level.

What's so Bad About Being Overweight?

African American women don't have the same hangups about their weight that women of many other ethnic groups seem to suffer. Most of us don't equate attractiveness with supermodel thinness, and are often comfortable with the fullness of our hips and the roundness of our bodies. But looks aside, there is clear evidence that excess body weight is hazardous to health. Even small, extra amounts raise the risk of four killer illnesses: heart disease, high blood pressure, diabetes, and cancer. Black women are at the greatest risk—60 percent are more likely to become obese than our white counterparts. Extra pounds take quality and years from our lives.

Don't waste more time by starting a crash diet, swallowing diet pills, or drinking some formula or potion; quick fixes don't cut it. Lasting results come with adopting an eating plan you can stay on for the rest of your life. To lose weight and keep it off, follow a diet that is low in fat, moderate in protein, and high in fiber-rich foods such as vegetables, fruits, and grains.

Regular exercise also plays a major role in maintaining healthy body weight. The best activities are those that raise heart and breathing rates, such as walking, running, bicycling (both stationary and regular), dancing, and jumping rope. Just 15 to 30 uninterrupted minutes of these aerobic activities repeated at least three times a week bring noticeable results in not only physical appearance but alertness, energy, agility, and even the ability to handle stress. A disciplined approach to diet and exercise improves blood chemistry and the heart's ability to accomplish the same amount of work with less effort.

Make yourself a promise to get rid of the extra weight.

Shaping Up Old Favorites

Time-honored recipes handed down from one generation to the next or from one club member or church sister to another become prized possessions. If you have such a recipe that's now showing its age—high in fat, cholesterol, calories, and/or sodium—you can bring those numbers down while adding to the fiber, vitamin, and mineral content of the dish. To hold on to the qualities that make the dish appealing in the first place, don't try too many changes at once—focus on just one or two ingredients. Use the following easy methods to put a fresh, healthful spin on old standbys.

- Cut the amount of solid fat or oil called for by one-fourth. If the results are pleasing, reduce down to one-half and so on.
- Use turkey breast in recipes calling for beef or veal. For chili, meatballs, and meat loaf, use ground turkey in place of ground beef.
- Increase the ratio of vegetables to meat in casseroles, stews, soups, and chili.
- Remove the skin from poultry before cooking.
- Choose low-fat or nonfat versions of dairy products. Most dairy items now offer a range of reduced-fat choices.

A Feast for the Eyes as Well as the Body

A good meal delights our senses of sight, smell, and taste. The familiar saying "The eye eats first" is true—just the sight of palatable food starts the mouth watering even before it opens. Build in eye appeal by planning your menu with an interplay of colors, shapes, and textures. Then use cooking techniques that keep foods appetizing. Overcooked vegetables appear pale and lifeless; fish, poultry, and baked goods look dried out.

Set the table. Nothing fancy, just the basics and touches that help create a comfortable and pleasant experience. To each plate or platter, add a small edible garnish, such as cherry tomatoes, lime wedges, or sprigs of the fresh herb used in preparing the dish. And don't push that sprig of parsley to the side—eat it. Parsley has lots of vitamin C and freshens the breath beautifully.

The Comfort of Soup

STONE SOUP is one of my favorite folktales. The first time I heard the story, I was seated cross-legged on the floor with the rest of my grade-school class. We listened with the rapt attention reserved only for storytime as our teacher, Mrs. Tedesco, read the book aloud. STONE SOUP left such an impression that to this day, cooking and the good feelings it stirs seem a bit magical to me.

You may recall the story of a road-weary traveler who arrives in a small village seeking food and shelter. Unable to find either, he boasts of his ability to make soup from a stone. He borrows a cauldron and fills it with water in which he places a polished stone. As the villagers gather to watch the spectacle, each becomes involved and adds a little—a piece of fish, a yam, half a cabbage, an onion, a pinch of seasoning—to the simmering cauldron. Before their eyes, the pot slowly fills with a fragrant and robust soup. Everyone is amazed to see what a grand meal has come from a mere stone and communal gifts. Hearts are opened and spirits rekindled. After spending the night as an honored guest, the traveler carefully packs his stone and heads toward the next village.

The world over, nothing satisfies like homemade soup. From simple broths to sumptuous gumbos, soups both nurture and nourish us. To enjoy quick, healthful meals throughout the week, cook a big batch of soup on the weekend or whenever time permits. You'll discover that some soups actually taste better when refrigerated overnight, after flavors have had a chance to mingle and marry. Lunching on the go? Soup travels well; take along a thermos filled with hot homemade soup and savor a delectable midday meal at your office, school, or favorite outdoor spot.

In updating cherished old recipes, I use broth as one of my key ingredients for layering flavors. Cooking rice, vegetables, fish, and other foods in broth instead of water enhances

All-purpose Vegetable Broth

◆

Basic Chicken Broth

◆

Old-fashioned Chicken Soup

◆

Seafood and Sausage Gumbo

◆

Salmon-Corn Chowder

◆

Shrimp Bisque

◆

Charleston She-Crab Soup

◆

Southern Peanut
(Groundnut) Soup

◆

Cuban Black Bean Soup
with Coriander Cream

◆

Butter Bean Soup

◆

Bountiful Vegetable Soup

◆

Cabbage and Ham Bone Soup

◆

Soup Garnishes and
Accompaniments

◆

Croutons

the inherent taste of the food. Canned broths are convenient and easy to use, but I find most to be extremely salty. And while the new fat-reduced and no-salt-added versions are a clear improvement, I can honestly say that none touch the flavor of homemade. If you're cooking up a batch, remember that broth will keep for up to three days in the refrigerator. Bring it to a boil first if you've held it a day or two longer. For broth anytime you want it, freeze some in ice-cube trays, then pop the cubes into a heavy-duty food storage bag.

To enhance the flavor of soups, try one or more of the following: low-fat, low-sodium stocks and broths; balsamic, red, or white wine vinegar; lemon juice; dry wines; multicolored peppercorns in mill (for fresh grinding); dried shrimp (ground); fresh garlic; vegetable purées; and assorted fresh and dried herbs, such as oregano, marjoram, and/or thyme.

Turn any of the following soups into a real meal by serving them with warm corn bread. To make corn muffins, hoecakes, or other crusty breads to sop up the last drop of juice, turn to the "Bread Basket" chapter. Garnishes to top off your soup, and easy directions for homemade croutons, are at the end of this chapter.

◆ Degrease the stock. If you use canned broth, refrigerate the unopened can until chilled; then remove the lid and lift off and discard the solidified fat. In the same way, refrigerate your bowl or jar of homemade broth, then lift off the top coating with a spoon. The result is a near-fat-free broth with just a few calories.

◆ Skim any fat off surface of soup. Because fats are lighter than water, most of the fat used to prepare soup or extracted from the ingredients while cooking will float to the top. Skim as you see fat accumulate, or refrigerate as above.

◆ Precook (sauté) vegetables such as onions, garlic, and celery in little or no fat. Although olive oil, butter, or margarine can bring out the best in these aromatic vegetables, cooking fat can be cut back dramatically with tasty results. Use I tablespoon OR LESS of fat and add a small amount of broth to prevent sticking.

◆ Rely on starchy vegetables, grains, and beans to cook down and add "creaminess." For added body, purée a portion of the soup in a blender or food processor and reheat with the rest of the soup.

◆ Add a ham bone or turkey carcass to the soup pot to impart meaty flavor without adding much fat. Any fat that's released during cooking can be skimmed from the surface.

Fat Chat
Don't let a fat attack ruin your pot. A hearty soup brimming with only wholesome, heartwarming ingredients brings joy to your kitchen table.

All-purpose Vegetable Broth

I chose this recipe to kick off this cookbook because it's a staple of good eating. Flavored with a cornucopia of vegetables, this light broth can be used as a backbone or first stage for other homemade soups, or as a seasoning for a wide variety of dishes. Or simply enjoy it as is, sipping as you would a mug of aromatic tea. Allow my recipe to inspire you—the ingredients and amounts indicated are only a suggestion. You can use more or less, toss in other items you like or whatever you happen to have on hand.

PER CUP (ESTIMATED)

CALORIES: 4
PROTEIN: 0 grams
FAT: 0 grams
SODIUM: 10 milligrams
CHOLESTEROL: 0 milligrams

◆ ABOUT 8 CUPS

3 ribs celery, broken or sliced thick
4 medium-sized unpeeled carrots, sliced thick
2 medium-sized turnips, peeled and sliced
2 medium-sized leeks, trimmed, carefully rinsed, and sliced
2 tomatoes, chopped coarse
1 large onion, stuck with several whole cloves
1 small bulb (whole head) garlic, unpeeled, sliced in half crosswise
5 to 6 sprigs fresh parsley
2 large bay leaves
1 tablespoon black peppercorns
1 teaspoon salt (optional)

1. In large pot or stockpot, combine all ingredients. Add enough water to cover, about 4 quarts. Over medium-high heat, bring to boil. Reduce heat to low; partially cover and cook at low simmer about 1½ hours. Using slotted spoon, remove and discard vegetables and herbs.

2. Pour broth through strainer or sieve lined with cheesecloth into jars or storage containers with tight lids. Discard solids left in cheesecloth. Let broth cool; cover jars or bowl securely and refrigerate up to 2 or 3 days until time to use.

Basic Chicken Broth

◆ 6 CUPS

4 pounds chicken parts, such as backs and necks
2 medium-sized carrots, sliced coarse
2 large celery stalks with leaves attached, sliced coarse
2 small turnips, peeled and chopped coarse
1 large onion, peeled, chopped coarse
2 to 4 parsley sprigs
2 bay leaves
½ teaspoon dried thyme leaves
1 teaspoon salt (optional)
10 peppercorns or ½ teaspoon freshly ground black pepper

1. In large pot or stockpot, combine chicken parts, carrots, celery, turnips, and onion, and cover with water. Over medium-high heat, bring to boil. Lower heat, cover, and simmer gently about 1 hour, skimming foam from top of stock frequently during first 30 minutes.

2. Add parsley, bay leaves, thyme, salt (if you like), and peppercorns. Partially cover pot with lid. Over low heat, simmer 1 additional hour, stirring occasionally. Remove chicken and vegetables with slotted spoon. Using large, shallow spoon, skim fat from top of stock and discard.

3. Pour broth through fine strainer; press solids to extract as much flavor and liquid as possible. You should have about 6 cups of liquid. If more has evaporated, add a bit of water. If there is too much liquid, boil down until only about 6 cups remain. For completely fat-free stock, refrigerate overnight. Then use a large, shallow spoon to lift off and discard solid fat. Stock may be refrigerated 2 or 3 days or frozen up to 6 months.

Once you discover the pleasing flavor this broth imparts, and its versatility, you'll use it time and again. And what a practical way to recycle chicken backs, necks, and wing tips. Remove these bony parts from whole chickens and collect them in a bag in the freezer until stock-making time.

PER CUP

CALORIES: **23**
PROTEIN: **2 grams**
FAT: **1 gram**
SODIUM: **65 milligrams**
CHOLESTEROL: **0 milligrams**

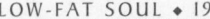

Old-fashioned Chicken Soup

The often maligned, yet noble, yard bird is central to an even healthier version of the soup served by grandmas everywhere as a cure-all for whatever ails you—in body, mind, or spirit. For a variation, try chicken-rice soup by substituting half a cup of uncooked rice for the noodles. And don't hesitate to throw in green peas, broccoli, or other favorite vegetables. Fresh produce can strengthen this soup's restorative powers.

PER SERVING

CALORIES: **242**
PROTEIN: **21 grams**
FAT: **5 grams**
SODIUM: **143 milligrams**
CHOLESTEROL: **36 milligrams**

◆ 6 SERVINGS

2 teaspoons vegetable oil
1 cup chopped onions
1 cup chopped carrots
1 cup chopped celery with leaves
6 cups Basic Chicken Broth (page 19)
¼ teaspoon dried thyme leaves
¼ teaspoon dried sage leaves
1 bay leaf
2 cups coarsely chopped mushrooms
½ teaspoon salt (optional)
½ teaspoon ground black or white pepper
¼ cup minced fresh flat-leaf parsley or cilantro
6 ounces dried noodles, spaghetti, fettuccine, or linguine
2 cups shredded chicken left from making broth or 2 cups chopped chicken breasts or thighs

1. In large pot, heat vegetable oil; add onions, carrots, and celery. Cook over medium heat, stirring frequently, until lightly browned, about 3 to 4 minutes.

2. Add broth; bring to boil. Stir in thyme, sage, and bay leaf. Add mushrooms, salt (if desired), pepper, parsley, noodles, and chicken. Reduce heat; simmer until noodles are tender. Discard bay leaf.

Gumbo

Multiculturalism, one of today's buzzwords, was a way of life in eighteenth-century New Orleans. The Choctaw Indians, French, Spanish, and Italians all contributed ingredients to this thick, stewlike dish created by the Africans. The name gumbo is a derivative of an African word for okra. Gumbo can contain any of many ingredients, including tomatoes, onions, one or several meats or shellfish such as chicken, ham, crab, crawfish, shrimp, or oysters. Common to all authentic gumbos is a dark roux, which adds incomparably rich flavor. Okra serves to thicken the mixture, as does filé powder; the one rule of gumbo making seems to be to add one or the other, never both.

One of the most famous gumbos is gumbo z'herbes—made with at least seven greens and served traditionally on Good Friday. In New Orleans, it seems every restaurant—from neighborhood dive to elegant white tablecloth establishment—serves gumbo. Olivier's, a fashionable yet cozy Creole restaurant in the French Quarter, features three types of gumbo on their daily menu. And if you can't decide which you'd like to try, you can order a sampler that includes all of them.

Seafood and Sausage Gumbo

The beauty of gumbo, aside from the jazzy dance it does on your taste buds, is that you can make it with whatever you have a hankering for. Treat this recipe as a guide to basic ingredients and proportions.

PER SERVING

CALORIES: **265**
PROTEIN: **23 grams**
FAT: **8 grams**
SODIUM: **336 milligrams**
CHOLESTEROL: **105 milligrams**

◆ 12 SERVINGS

2 tablespoons vegetable oil
¼ cup unbleached all-purpose flour
2 garlic cloves, minced
1 large yellow onion, chopped fine
2 ribs celery, sliced thin
1 medium-sized green bell pepper, seeded and diced
2 1-pound cans whole tomatoes with juice, chopped
1 bay leaf
1 teaspoon hot pepper sauce
6 cups reduced-fat Basic Chicken Broth (page 19)
1½ pounds raw medium-sized shrimp, shelled and deveined
1 pound fresh lump crabmeat
½ pint fresh oysters with juice
½ pound low-fat kielbasa or smoked sausage, cut into ¼-inch-thick slices
¼ cup chopped fresh parsley
4 or 5 scallions (including green tops), sliced
2 teaspoons filé powder
1 teaspoon salt (optional)
1 teaspoon freshly ground black pepper
4 cups hot cooked rice

1. Heat vegetable oil in stockpot over low heat. Stir in flour until blended. Make roux by cooking slowly and stirring mixture until it is rich brown in color.

2. Add garlic, onion, celery, and bell pepper; cook and stir just until vegetables soften. Stir in tomatoes with juice, bay leaf, and hot pepper sauce; cook about 5 minutes. Stir in chicken broth, shrimp, crabmeat, and oysters with juice; simmer 5 minutes.

3. Meanwhile, in nonstick skillet, cook smoked sausage until browned around edges; pour off fat. To simmering mixture, add sausage, parsley, scallions, filé powder, salt (if desired), and black pepper. Simmer 5 additional minutes. Spoon rice into soup bowls; ladle gumbo over rice.

THE CREOLE SECRET

"First you make a roux," a New Orleans local said, letting me in on the oft-repeated secret of authentic Creole cooking. From the French Quarter to bayou country, good cooks speak of roux in tones of reverence. Fortunately for us, a roux is simply a mixture of fat and flour cooked until browned. The color can range from light golden to deep mahogany—the deeper the hue, the more pronounced the flavor. A cast-iron skillet or kettle, which distributes heat more evenly, maximizes your control when browning. The standard one-to-one ratio of flour and fat can be changed to one-to-one-half with beautiful results. The trick is to keep the roux moving by stirring constantly in a circular motion and pushing the roux from the bottom of the skillet. Use a Flame Tamer and a watchful eye to keep the mixture from burning. A burned roux cannot be salvaged—you're better off throwing it out and starting over.

Salmon-Corn Chowder

This homey chowder stretches the luxurious taste of fresh salmon to make an indulgence more affordable. Salmon is an excellent source of omega-3 fatty acids. These polyunsaturated fatty acids are the "good" kind that are associated with reducing the risk of heart disease. Serve this wonderful soup as a main dish of a luncheon when you're catching up on the times with a friend.

PER SERVING

CALORIES: **271**
PROTEIN: **14 grams**
FAT: **6 grams**
SODIUM: **213 milligrams**
CHOLESTEROL: **15 milligrams**

◆ 5 SERVINGS

3 cups peeled, diced (¼- to ½-inch cubes) boiling potatoes
½ teaspoon salt (optional)
2 cups 2-percent-fat milk
1 cup minced onion
2 teaspoons tub-style margarine
1 cup clam juice
½ pound salmon steak
1 tablespoon fresh lemon juice
1 tablespoon unbleached all-purpose flour
¼ teaspoon ground white pepper
1 cup corn cut from cob or frozen whole-kernel corn, thawed
2 tablespoons snipped fresh dill

1. In large saucepan, combine potatoes, ¼ teaspoon salt (if desired), and milk; bring to low simmer. Cook until potatoes are almost tender, about 10 minutes. Set aside.

2. In dutch oven or pot over low heat, cook onion with margarine until softened. Stir in ½ cup clam juice. Place salmon skin-side-down on top of onion; sprinkle with remaining ¼ teaspoon salt (if desired) and lemon juice. Cover and gently cook salmon until it is opaque at thickest part and begins to flake, about 8 to 10 minutes. Using slotted spoon, lift salmon from bed of onion and transfer to plate.

3. Sprinkle flour and pepper over onion; cook, stirring, for about 3 minutes. Stir in remaining ½ cup clam juice, milk-potato mixture, and corn; simmer, stirring occasionally, about 5 minutes.

4. Meanwhile, carefully remove and discard skin and bones from salmon; break into large chunks. Add salmon and dill to pot. Over medium heat, cook until heated through.

Shrimp Bisque

Thick, creamy texture distinguishes a bisque from all other seafood soups and chowders. Ever-so-lightly spiked with sherry or dry white wine, a bisque adds a certain sophistication to the first course for a dinner party.

PER SERVING

CALORIES: 161
PROTEIN: 12 grams
FAT: 5 grams
SODIUM: 254 milligrams
CHOLESTEROL: 74 milligrams

◆ 8 SERVINGS

- 1 tablespoon olive oil
- 1 pound medium-sized shrimp, shelled (keep shells) and deveined
- 1 tablespoon light butter or margarine
- 1 onion, diced
- 1 carrot, chopped
- 1 celery rib, chopped
- 2 cups clam juice, fish stock, or chicken broth
- 1 cup dry white wine
- 2 tablespoons tomato paste
- ¼ cup uncooked long-grain rice
- 1 teaspoon dried thyme
- 1 bay leaf
- ½ teaspoon salt (optional)
- ¼ teaspoon cayenne pepper
- 2 cups 2-percent-fat milk

1. In 4-quart dutch oven, heat olive oil over medium-high heat; cook shrimp shells, stirring constantly, until pink. Using slotted spoon, remove shells, leaving flavored oil in pot. Add shrimp to oil; cook, stirring frequently, until shrimp turn pink, about 3 minutes. Transfer cooked shrimp to bowl.

2. In same pot, heat butter, onion, carrot, and celery. Cook and stir until tender. Stir in clam juice, wine, and tomato paste; simmer about 5 minutes. Add rice, thyme, bay leaf, salt (if desired), and cayenne; reduce heat to low. Cover and simmer until rice is tender, about 15 minutes.

3. Remove pot from heat. Discard bay leaf. Stir in cooked shrimp. In covered blender container, purée half of mixture at a time. Return puréed shrimp mixture to pot; stir in milk until blended. Over medium heat, bring to simmer. Serve hot.

Charleston She-Crab Soup

My first bowl of this classic soup was from the kitchen of Edna Lewis, cookbook author, chef, and legend. It was exquisite! After that I would order the South Carolina classic whenever I spotted it on a menu—only to be disappointed. Over the years, however, I've come up with this rendition. Inspired by Edna but free of heavy cream and bacon, it highlights the sweet lushness of crabmeat. Why is the she-crab the star of this soup? She comes with a bonus— her delightful roe, which delivers its own richness. Buy live and kicking crabs and cook them, or buy already steamed crabs and you may find roe. (The females are the ones wearing the full aprons.) Or use lump crabmeat.

PER SERVING

CALORIES: **231**
PROTEIN: **27 grams**
FAT: **4 grams**
SODIUM: **430 milligrams**
CHOLESTEROL: **85 milligrams**

◆ 6 SERVINGS

 1 tablespoon light butter
 3 tablespoons unbleached all-purpose flour
 3 cups evaporated skim milk
 2 cups fish stock or clam juice
 ½ teaspoon salt (optional)
 ¼ teaspoon ground nutmeg
 ¼ teaspoon paprika
 ¼ teaspoon cayenne pepper
 1 tablespoon chopped fresh parsley
 1 teaspoon minced fresh chives
 1 pound lump crabmeat (from female crabs if possible), picked free of all shell and cartilage
 ¼ cup dry sherry

1. In dutch oven over low heat, melt butter. Add flour and cook just until flour starts to brown, about 1 to 2 minutes. Slowly add milk, stirring rapidly until liquid has thickened, about 3 minutes.

2. Add stock, salt, nutmeg, paprika, cayenne, parsley, and chives; simmer for 5 minutes. Flake in crabmeat and stir to mix. Stir in sherry; ladle into tureen or soup bowl. Serve immediately.

Southern Peanut (Groundnut) Soup

◆ 6 SERVINGS

1 tablespoon peanut oil

1 medium-sized yellow onion, chopped fine

2 large celery ribs, chopped fine

2 garlic cloves, minced

2 tablespoons unbleached all-purpose flour

5 to 6 cups Basic Chicken Broth (page 19)

1 cup creamy natural peanut butter

½ cup evaporated skim milk

¼ teaspoon salt (optional)

¼ teaspoon freshly ground black pepper

1 teaspoon hot red pepper flakes

Optional garnishes: chopped chives and chopped unsalted roasted peanuts

1. In large pot, heat peanut oil over medium heat. Add onion and celery; cook until translucent, about 10 minutes. Stir in garlic. Using whisk, mix in flour until all vegetables are coated and mixture is pastelike. Cook 2 to 3 minutes (do not brown flour).

2. Still using whisk, stir in about 2¾ cups stock, mixing well. In mixing bowl, whisk 2¾ cups stock into peanut butter; stir until blended. Increase heat to medium. Add peanut butter mixture to pot, whisking constantly until soup is well mixed and has come to boil. Reduce heat to low; simmer 20 minutes.

3. Blend in milk, salt (if desired), black pepper, and red pepper flakes. (If soup is too thick, stir in a bit more stock.) Garnish with chives and chopped nuts if you wish.

Note: For even more flavor and texture, add cubed or pureed cooked sweet potatoes after stirring in the peanut butter.

Peanuts are called groundnuts because that's where they grow! Groundnuts are a reliable source of rich protein in West African diets and appear in a number of dishes. The soups often contain poultry, beef, or yams. This soup of remarkable flavors was handed down from our West African ancestors to our forebears in the southern United States, evidence of an unbroken culinary link.

PER SERVING

CALORIES: **321**
PROTEIN: **16 grams**
FAT: **23 grams**
SODIUM: **136 milligrams**
CHOLESTEROL: **138 milligrams**

Cuban Black-Bean Soup with Coriander Cream

For an earthy vegetarian soup, cook the beans in vegetable broth and omit the turkey ham. Swirl herbed cream on top for flair and flavor.

◆ 6 SERVINGS

  2 cups dried black beans (turtle beans)
  8 cups cold water or vegetable, chicken, or beef broth or combination of water and broth
  1 tablespoon olive oil
½-pound piece turkey ham, diced
  1 large yellow onion, chopped
  3 garlic cloves, minced
  2 teaspoons chili powder
  1 teaspoon dried thyme
  1 teaspoon dried oregano
  1 teaspoon ground cumin (or to taste)
  1 teaspoon salt (optional)
  1 teaspoon crushed dried hot red pepper
  1 large bay leaf
  ¼ cup dark rum or dry sherry
  ⅓ cup low-fat sour cream
  ¼ cup chopped fresh cilantro (coriander) leaves
  1 tablespoon fresh lime juice
Optional garnishes: sprigs of cilantro, chopped fresh tomato, finely chopped hard-cooked eggs, thinly sliced lemon

1. In large bowl or colander, rinse beans thoroughly with cold running water, picking through and discarding damaged beans and any debris. In large bowl or dutch oven, cover beans with about 1 quart cold water; soak overnight. Drain beans and discard water.

2. In dutch oven or large pot, combine beans and 8 cups fresh water or broth or combination. Over low heat, simmer until very tender, about 2 hours. Stir occasionally from bottom.

3. Meanwhile, in medium-sized nonstick skillet, heat olive oil; sauté turkey ham and onion. Stir in garlic, chili powder, thyme, oregano, cumin, salt (if desired), hot red pepper, bay leaf, and ¼ cup water; simmer about 5 minutes. Stir ham and onion mixture into cooked beans and liquid. Partially cover and simmer until flavors are blended, about 10 minutes. Remove and discard bay leaf. Stir in rum.

4. To make coriander cream: In blender container or bowl, combine sour cream, cilantro, and lime juice; process or stir until blended. Set aside.

5. Ladle soup into tureen or bowls; spoon coriander cream in swirls on top. Garnish further as desired.

NOTE: To thicken and make creamier, purée half of soup in blender or food processor or by pressing through sieve. Stir purée back into soup pot; mix and reheat.

Butter Bean Soup

This creamy soup comes by its thick richness naturally. A type of large dried lima beans, butter beans offer a full supply of fiber and flavor. Turkey ham adds smoky flavor and manages to keep fat in check.

PER SERVING

CALORIES: **258**
PROTEIN: **20 grams**
FAT: **2 grams**
SODIUM: **260 milligrams**
CHOLESTEROL: **11 milligrams**

◆ 6 SERVINGS

1 pound dried butter beans
1 cup diced turkey ham
2 celery ribs, sliced thin
3 medium-sized scallions (including green tops), chopped
2 teaspoons thyme
6 cups Basic Chicken Broth (page 19)
4 cups water
Optional garnish: chopped fresh tomatoes

1. In large bowl or colander, rinse beans thoroughly with cold running water, picking through and discarding damaged beans and any debris. In large bowl, with enough water to cover, soak beans overnight. Or, to QUICK soak: Place beans and water in large kettle and bring to boil over high heat. Reduce heat to medium and let beans boil 1 minute. Remove from heat; let stand 1 hour covered with lid. Drain beans.

2. In large kettle combine all ingredients, except garnish, cover and simmer until beans are soft and tender, about 1½ to 2 hours, depending upon size. For added creaminess, a portion of the soup can be puréed in a food processor or blender, then stirred back into the pot and heated. Serve piping hot; garnish with chopped tomatoes.

Bountiful Vegetable Soup

◆ 6 SERVINGS

  1 tablespoon vegetable oil

  2 onions, chopped coarse

  2 celery ribs, chopped coarse

  2 garlic cloves, minced

  1 tablespoon fresh thyme or 1 teaspoon dried thyme

  1 bay leaf

  6 cups All-purpose Vegetable Broth (page 18)

28- ounce can whole tomatoes, undrained, chopped coarse

  2 carrots, cut into ¼-inch-thick slices

  2 cups cut string beans, about 1½ inches long
    (strings removed)

  2 white potatoes, peeled and diced

16-ounce can garbanzo beans, drained and rinsed; or about
    2 cups other cooked beans

In nonstick dutch oven or kettle, heat vegetable oil over medium-high heat; cook and stir onion, celery, and garlic until onion is transparent, about 4 to 5 minutes. Stir in thyme and bay leaf. Stir in broth, tomatoes, carrots, string beans, and potatoes. Reduce heat to low simmer; cook about 15 minutes. Stir in garbanzo beans; heat through. Remove and discard bay leaf. Ladle into tureen or large soup bowls.

A piece of warm corn bread or crusty peasant bread completes this feast in a bowl. It will leave you full, satisfied, and pleased to know that you've put left-over vegetables to good use. Add corn, black-eyed peas, chopped collards, or any other perfectly good vegetable lounging around your fridge.

PER SERVING

CALORIES: **223**

PROTEIN: **7 grams**

FAT: **4 grams**

SODIUM: **447 milligrams**

CHOLESTEROL: **0 milligrams**

Cabbage and Ham Bone Soup

The flavors of cabbage and ham are a traditional pairing, and there's no need to break the two up after all these years. The ham that clings to the bone is more than enough to add a classic taste to this stick-to-your-ribs soup.

PER SERVING

CALORIES: **63**
PROTEIN: **4 grams**
FAT: **1 gram**
SODIUM: **163 milligrams**
CHOLESTEROL: **2 milligrams**

◆ 8 SERVINGS

Nonstick cooking spray
  1 medium-sized yellow onion, chopped
  1 stalk celery, sliced thin
  1 quart All-purpose Vegetable Broth (page 18) or low-sodium canned broth
  1 meaty cooked or roasted ham bone
  1 bay leaf
  2 large carrots, diced
  2 large white turnips, peeled and diced
  ½ green cabbage (about 1 pound), cored and chopped into 1-inch pieces or coarsely shredded (about 4 cups)
  2 tablespoons fresh lemon juice or cider vinegar
  ½ teaspoon freshly ground black pepper
  ⅛ teaspoon cayenne pepper
  1 teaspoon caraway seeds (optional)
Optional garnish: chopped or sliced flat-leaf parsley

1. In large pot coated with nonstick cooking spray, sauté onion and celery just until onion is transparent. Add broth, ham bone, and bay leaf; bring to simmer. Cook several minutes to season broth.

2. Stir in carrots, turnips, cabbage, lemon juice, black pepper, and cayenne. Simmer until vegetables are tender but not mushy, about 15 minutes. Remove ham bone and set aside until cool enough to handle. Meanwhile, using large, shallow spoon, skim and discard any fat from surface of soup. Remove and discard bay leaf.

3. Cut ham from bone and chop into small pieces; return meat to soup pot. Stir in caraway seeds if you wish; mix well. Cook just until heated through. Ladle into tureen or bowls; sprinkle with parsley and serve.

Soup Garnishes and Accompaniments

Garnishes dress up what otherwise might be a plain-looking soup, or they add pizzazz to one that's already pretty. A sprinkle of contrasting color and texture heightens eye and taste appeal. Go easy, of course, to keep fat and calories in check. To prevent a garnish from sinking to the bottom of the tureen or bowl, simply float it atop a thin slice of toasted French bread. Dollops of whipped topping, sour cream, or yogurt are made even more attractive when sprinkled with chopped fresh herbs, paprika, or curry powder.

For a different approach, place a toasted slice of French bread in the bottom of each soup bowl, then ladle the soup over it.

BACON-FLAVORED BITS—purchase from natural-food stores

BASIL LEAVES—sliced

CARROT—shredded or julienned

CHEESE—shredded

CILANTRO—chopped

CROUTONS—(page 34)

CUCUMBER—seeded, then shredded or julienned

HARD-COOKED EGG—sieved, chopped, or thinly sliced

LEMON SLICES—sliced paper-thin

MUSHROOMS—whole enoki or larger mushrooms sliced thin or julienned

PAPRIKA—sprinkled

PARMESAN CHEESE—freshly grated

SCALLION (including green tops)—chopped with diced red bell pepper

SOUR CREAM (low-fat)—dollop or swirl in

TOMATO—diced fresh

TORTILLA CHIPS—crumbled

Croutons

Place a bowl or basket of these crunchy cubes of bread on the table to sprinkle over soup just before eating. Use your choice of sliced bread—white, dark, or multigrained. Cubes of corn bread or focaccia (thick Italian bread seasoned with olive oil and herbs) also make delicious croutons. Simply broil bread cubes for the lightest, no-fat-added topping.

◆ MAKES ABOUT 2 CUPS

4 slices bread
1 teaspoon vegetable oil
1 teaspoon margarine

Trim crusts from bread. Using sharp knife, cut bread crosswise, then lengthwise, to form small, even-sized cubes.

TO PAN-FRY: In large nonstick skillet, heat oil and margarine; add bread cubes. Cook, stirring constantly, until crisp and golden.

TO BAKE: Heat oven to 375°F. Mix oil and margarine; brush bread slices very lightly (2 teaspoons don't go far). Cut into cubes as described above. On baking sheet or in large shallow pan, spread cubes in single layer. Bake, turning a few times, until evenly browned. Or omit fat and simply toast until dry and golden.

TO BROIL: Spread bread cubes in shallow pan and broil until toasted. Watch carefully lest they burn.

NOTE: Do not add oil to corn bread or focaccia croutons.

Víbrant Vegetables and Dríed Beans

In the South, vegetables were never incidental to the meal or added to the plate merely as an afterthought. Instead, just-picked, boldly flavored vegetables truly epitomized down-home cooking. The greens, okra, black-eyed peas, and yams that traveled with us from Africa soon flourished in our fields and gardens here. We intuitively combined them with green beans, squash, tomatoes, corn, and other local vegetables and grains to create delectable dishes destined to become regional classics.

Our love of vegetables is also expressed in the Caribbean, where open-air markets feature almost overwhelmingly spectacular displays of fresh produce. Piled high in architectural pyramids or arranged in handwoven baskets on tables or colorful cloths on the ground are eggplants, pumpkins, cho cho (christophene, chayote, mirliton), other squash, pigeon peas, black beans, plantains, avocados, ginger, and all manner of sweet and hot peppers. The produce is most often sold by women who left their homes in the countryside before the crack of dawn to bring in their small harvest.

The same technologies that have made the world smaller have also vastly increased our market choices. Thus, vegetables grown in St. Croix may be enjoyed for dinner in St. Louis. We can revel in Chinese cabbages from California, sugar snap peas from Guatemala, and turtle beans from southern Mexico, not to mention spaghetti squash, broccoli rabe, jicama, kale, turnips, rutabagas, and zucchini—all adding wondrous flavors and variety to meals.

Maybe you've noticed that meatless meals are no longer just for vegetarians. Many people seeking a healthier way of eating forgo meat one or two days a week. For a splendid vegetarian meal, prepare two or three of the vegetable side dishes from this chapter, including at least one deeply colored vegetable. To set forth a grand feast or vegetarian buffet table,

Collard Greens with
Sun-dried Tomatoes

◆

Smothered Cabbage

◆

Southern Succotash

◆

Miss Bertha's Corn Pudding

◆

Simple Baked Sweet Potatoes

◆

Orange Sweet Potato Soufflé

◆

Honey-Pineapple Glazed Yams

◆

Grilled Sweet Potatoes

◆

Mashed Rutabagas
and Potatoes

◆

Garlic Mashed Potatoes

◆

Oven "Fried" Okra

◆

Picnic Potato Salad

◆

Turnip Tops and Bottoms

◆

Moroccan Vegetable Stew

◆

Fresh Field Peas with
Whole Okra

◆

Fireball Vegetable Chili

◆

Brazilian Black Beans with
Marinated Tomatoes

◆

Black-eyed Pea Salad with
Lemon Vinaigrette

◆

Buttermilk Salad Dressing

make four or more vegetable dishes, including a starchy one, one that is deep green, a deep yellow or orange vegetable, plus one grain dish. If this is not already your eating style, you'll discover that meatless meals need not be equated with lack of flavor and boredom. But don't take my word for it.

"And God said, Behold, I have given you every herb bearing seed, which is upon the face of all the earth, and every tree, in the which is the fruit of a tree yielding seed; to you it shall for meat." (Genesis 1:29, King James Version)

The vegetables in this chapter use herbs, spices, and a variety of ingredients to give flavor without fat. Adding more vegetables to your diet could be one of the biggest steps you can take toward better health.

Fat Chat
Vegetables are naturally low in fat and contain zero cholesterol.

◆ Move away from home-style cooking with meat. Salt pork (cured fat), fatback (fresh fat that comes from the back instead of the belly of the pig), or ham hocks (ankles) were traditionally added to bolster flavor and fortify an often meager diet. Now we know better. The natural flavor of vegetables can stand on its own or receive more healthful enhancement from broth or bouillon cubes, herbs, and/or aromatic vegetables such as onion, garlic, and shallots.

◆ Hold the fries. When potatoes, onion rings, and zucchini are fried, they aren't much better for you than potato chips. Just ten French fries add up to 8 grams of fat. Select low-fat cooking methods. Real mashed potatoes go well with sandwiches as well as with dinner entrées; add just a small amount of light butter, or leave it out and add low-fat milk, herbs, or garlic for flavor.

◆ Add bell peppers for extra taste and color appeal. Bell peppers perk up vegetable dishes. Instead of the familiar green version, substitute red, yellow, orange, or even purple bell peppers. (During summer months, colored bells are about the same price as green.)

◆ Splash on vinegar. Flavored vinegars, such as raspberry, tarragon, red wine, or chili pepper, or aged vinegars such as balsamic, add zest to vegetables.

◆ Toss in a bouquet garni. This French term describes a convenient, retrievable little pouch of herbs and seasonings added to soups, stews, dried beans, and vegetables to impart flavor. To make one quickly, lay 2 bay leaves, several peppercorns, whole cloves, parsley stems, and a sprig of fresh thyme on a 6-inch square of cheesecloth; tie ends together or bind with string and add to pot.

◆ Reverse your homemade salad dressing ratio. Switch from the traditional three parts oil and one part vinegar to three parts acid (lemon juice, tomato juice, vinegar) and one part oil, or equal amounts of each.

Collard Greens with Sun-dried Tomatoes

At least one new cookbook arrives at my desk each workday. When a little book entitled SUN-DRIED TOMATOES turned up, I mused that it must be the last, as all possible cookbook subjects were now covered. Glancing through it, however, I was struck by the versatility of dried tomatoes and became curious as to how they would taste in place of the fresh tomatoes I usually add to greens. The experiment paid off. Dried tomatoes are intense, as are greens—the interplay of flavors is superb. Because of the effort that goes into preparing fresh greens and the excitement they generate among those lucky enough to partake, it's practical to make a large batch.

PER SERVING

CALORIES: 133
PROTEIN: 5 grams
FAT: 4 grams
SODIUM: 105 milligrams
CHOLESTEROL: 0 milligrams

◆ 8 SERVINGS

4 pounds small young collard greens
2 cups Basic Chicken Broth or All-purpose Vegetable Broth (pages 18, 19)
2 tablespoons safflower oil or olive oil
1 large yellow onion, chopped
3 garlic cloves, minced
10 sun-dried tomatoes (no salt or sulfur added), sliced
2 tablespoons balsamic vinegar or cider vinegar
1 tablespoon brown sugar
1 fresh hot chile pepper, seeds and membranes removed, minced
1 teaspoon salt (optional)
½ teaspoon freshly ground black pepper

1. Pick through greens, discarding yellow leaves and thick stems; rinse thoroughly in several changes of water. One small batch at a time, stack and roll leaves into cigar shapes; slice crosswise into thin strips, or chop.

2. Place wet greens and broth in large kettle; bring to boil. Reduce heat to simmer and cook about 20 minutes; stir greens from bottom as they cook down.

3. Meanwhile, in large skillet, heat safflower or olive oil; add onion. Sauté about 5 minutes; add garlic and sauté about 2 additional minutes. Add tomatoes, vinegar, brown sugar, hot chile pepper, salt (if desired), and black pepper; sauté several minutes.

4. When greens are almost tender, stir in tomato mixture. Simmer, partially covered, about 15 minutes or until greens are of desired tenderness. Remove from heat; cover and let sit about 5 minutes before serving.

A GREEN NOTE

Grit is often the ruination of an otherwise good pot of greens. It takes patient attention to remove the dirt that loves to cling to the stems and leaves. Rinsing is not enough; a brief soaking is needed. Fill the sink with cold water and a sprinkle of salt. Add the greens and soak about 5 minutes. The dirt sinks and any crawlers are loosened. Lift the greens into a large bowl or basket. Clean the sink, then repeat this process at least twice. Remove the coarse portion of the stem from each leaf. "Picking" greens is an excellent job for children; it keeps their little fingers busy and helps them to understand how the raw becomes the cooked.

Smothered Cabbage

"Smothered" is a word used to describe any of a variety of dishes blanketed with a gravy while cooking, or (as in this dish) cooked in a covered skillet. Some believe the term may derive from the use of a weighted-down plate to cover the dish as it cooks. This recipe cooks the cabbage in just the rinsing water that clings and natural juices, leaving it tender, yet with body and texture. I sometimes sprinkle it with a pinch of caraway or dill seeds for an added taste sensation.

PER SERVING

CALORIES: **71**
PROTEIN: **3 grams**
FAT: **3 grams**
SODIUM: **28 milligrams**
CHOLESTEROL: **0 milligrams**

◆ 6 SIDE-DISH SERVINGS

1 small head green cabbage, wilted or yellow leaves removed
1 tablespoon vegetable oil
1 large yellow onion, chopped coarse
1 large green bell pepper, seeded and cut into strips or rings
1 teaspoon crushed red pepper
¼ teaspoon freshly ground black pepper
¼ teaspoon salt (optional)

Using a long, sharp knife, core the cabbage; chop into 1-inch pieces or shred coarse. Place in large colander; rinse with cold water. Heat vegetable oil in a large heavy skillet with a lid over medium-low heat. Sauté onion until light golden, about 10 minutes. Add cabbage and bell pepper; sprinkle with hot peppers and (if desired) salt. Press cabbage down with lid (add extra weight on top of lid if necessary to hold down). Cook, covered (stirring from bottom to top occasionally), until cabbage is tender but not mushy, about 25 minutes.

Southern Succotash

♦ 6 SERVINGS

  2 tablespoons vegetable oil
  1 large onion, chopped
  2 cups shelled fresh lima beans, or 10-ounce package baby
    lima beans
  1 large green bell pepper, seeds and membranes removed,
    chopped
  2 garlic cloves, chopped fine
  1 teaspoon salt (optional)
  1 teaspoon ground white pepper
Kernels from 4 ears yellow sweet corn, or 10-ounce package
    frozen corn, thawed
1½ pounds fresh okra, or 10-ounce package sliced okra
  2 tomatoes, quartered or chopped coarse

In large pot, heat vegetable oil and add onion; cook and stir about 5 minutes. Stir in shelled lima beans. Add 2 cups water and cook over medium heat for 10 minutes. Add bell pepper, garlic, salt (if desired), and white pepper. Stir in corn, okra, and tomatoes and let simmer until okra is tender, about 10 minutes.

Now an American classic, this combination of corn and lima beans was enjoyed by Native Americans long before the first European settlers came ashore. Succotash has many nuances. I'm sure African Americans were the first to add okra. Adapt this recipe to suit your taste or menu by scaling back to just the basics or adding chicken or other meat to create a thick stew.

PER SERVING

CALORIES: **224**
PROTEIN: **9 grams**
FAT: **6 grams**
SODIUM: **19 milligrams**
CHOLESTEROL: **0 milligrams**

Miss Bertha's Corn Pudding

One of the delights of summer eating is a fresh, creamy corn pudding. Bertha and Jim Jackson were members of our extended family who lived on a farm in Fenwick, Michigan. Because the sugar in corn starts to turn to starch as soon as the ear is picked from the stalk, Miss Bertha would put the water on to boil right before she went out to pick it. In this recipe the natural sweetness of the corn is enhanced by a small amount of added sugar. Always purchase corn the same day you intend to cook it. Corn pudding makes an exceptionally tasty side dish for grilled poultry and fish.

PER SERVING

CALORIES: **147**
PROTEIN: **5 grams**
FAT: **3 grams**
SODIUM: **67 milligrams**
CHOLESTEROL: **31 milligrams**

◆ 8 SERVINGS

8 ears yellow sweet corn, husks and silk removed, or about 2 cups frozen corn kernels
1 large egg, beaten slightly
2 cups skim or 1-percent-fat milk
2 tablespoons cornstarch
2 tablespoons granulated sugar
1 tablespoon melted butter or margarine
1 teaspoon salt (optional)
½ teaspoon freshly ground black pepper
½ teaspoon ground nutmeg
Optional garnish: minced fresh parsley

Preheat oven to 350°F. Using sharp knife, cut kernels and scrape "milk" from cob into a large, shallow bowl. Stir in egg, milk, cornstarch, sugar, butter, salt (if desired), pepper, and nutmeg until mixed. Pour mixture into greased 1½-quart baking dish. Bake until pudding is set, about 40 minutes. Sprinkle with parsley.

NOTE: To cut fresh kernels from the cob, stand the ear tip down in a shallow bowl. Use a sharp chef's knife and cut downward with a slight sawing motion. Then use the dull edge of the knife to scrape down the remaining pulp and "milk."

Simple Baked Sweet Potatoes

◆ 4 SERVINGS

4 medium-sized sweet potatoes

Preheat oven to 375°F. Using vegetable brush, scrub potatoes under running water; dry with paper towels. With fork or paring knife, prick potatoes in several areas. Place on ungreased baking pan or rack in center of oven. Bake until flesh is soft when tested with fork, about 45 minutes to an hour. To serve, make cut down potato center; pinch edges to release insides. Fluff with fork.

In a recent study, the Center for Science in the Public Interest ranked the sweet potato first in nutrition of all vegetables. This recipe is by far the easiest and most delicious way I know to prepare "sweets." It's rather amazing that the longer they bake, the sweeter they become.

PER POTATO

CALORIES: 117
PROTEIN: 2 grams
FAT: 0 grams
SODIUM: 11 milligrams
CHOLESTEROL: 0 milligrams

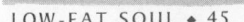

Orange Sweet Potato Soufflé

This regal dish (the top actually rises above the rim to form a burnished gold crown) deserves the undivided attention of your guests. That's why I suggest you serve it at a time when it will be noticed for all its glory and not upstaged by the flamboyance of a golden roasted turkey or a noisy celebration. The adage—guests must wait for the soufflé, as a soufflé will not wait for guests—still applies.

◆ 6 SERVINGS

- 3 tablespoons firmly packed brown sugar
- 1 tablespoon cornstarch
- ½ teaspoon ground nutmeg
- ⅛ teaspoon ground ginger
- 2 teaspoons grated orange zest
- ⅛ teaspoon salt (optional)
- ½ cup skim or 1-percent-fat milk
- ¼ cup orange juice
- 2 eggs, separated, plus 1 egg white
- 2 tablespoons melted butter or margarine
- 1 teaspoon pure vanilla extract
- 2 cups cooked, mashed sweet potatoes or yams

1. Preheat oven to 375°F. Grease bottom of 1½-quart soufflé dish or straight-sided casserole; set aside. In medium saucepan, mix brown sugar, cornstarch, nutmeg, ginger, orange zest, and (if desired) salt. Gradually stir in milk and orange juice until blended. Over medium heat, cook mixture, stirring constantly until thickened; remove from heat.

2. In small bowl, using fork, beat egg yolks well. Add small amount of hot milk mixture; mix well. Add yolk mixture to remaining hot milk mixture. Stir in butter, vanilla, and sweet potatoes.

3. In medium bowl, beat egg whites with rotary or electric mixer until stiff peaks form; carefully fold into sweet potato mixture. Pour into soufflé dish. (The dish should be no less than ¾ full.) Bake 40 minutes. Serve immediately.

Honey-Pineapple Glazed Yams

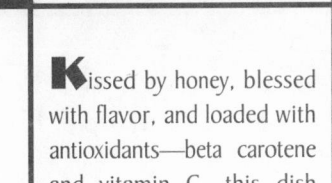

◆ 4 SERVINGS

4 medium-sized (about 6 ounces each) whole, unpeeled yams
¼ cup honey
¼ cup pineapple juice
2 teaspoons grated orange or lemon zest
½ teaspoon ground cardamom
½ teaspoon ground ginger

1. In dutch oven, cover yams with cold water; bring to boil. Reduce heat; simmer until just tender yet firm, about 20 minutes. Drain; set aside to cool slightly.

2. In same dutch oven, combine honey, pineapple juice, zest, cardamom, and ginger. Cook over low heat, stirring occasionally, until mixture is slightly reduced, about 10 minutes. Peel yams; cut into thick slices. Add yams to glaze; stir carefully to coat completely. Cook over low heat until yams are nicely glazed, about 25 minutes.

Kissed by honey, blessed with flavor, and loaded with antioxidants—beta carotene and vitamin C—this dish fosters good health and good eating.

PER SERVING

CALORIES: **271**
PROTEIN: **3 grams**
FAT: **0 grams**
SODIUM: **15 milligrams**
CHOLESTEROL: **0 milligrams**

Grilled Sweet Potatoes

Grilling the entire meal adds to the fun and ease of outdoor eating. Sweet potatoes are a natural for cookouts.

◆ 4 SERVINGS

4 large sweet potatoes
¼ cup melted light margarine
1 teaspoon salt (optional)
1 teaspoon ground black pepper

1. Prepare grill for cooking. Heat until coals are uniformly ashy gray in color, about 20 minutes. Scrub sweet potatoes under running water with vegetable brush. Cut into ½-inch-thick slices. Brush both sides with melted margarine (reserve remaining margarine); sprinkle lightly with salt (if desired) and pepper.

2. Arrange potatoes on grill rack; cook, turning and basting occasionally with margarine, until flesh is soft when pricked with fork, about 20 minutes.

Mashed Rutabagas and Potatoes

◆ ABOUT 6 SERVINGS

1 medium-sized rutabaga, peeled (they're usually covered with wax) and cut into 1-inch cubes

3 medium-sized russet potatoes, peeled and cut into 2-inch cubes

⅓ cup skim or 1-percent-fat milk

1 tablespoon margarine or butter

½ teaspoon salt (optional)

¼ teaspoon freshly ground white pepper

⅛ teaspoon freshly grated nutmeg

Optional garnish: chopped parsley

In large saucepan, bring about 2 cups water to boil. Add rutabaga and cook about 10 minutes. Add potatoes and cook vegetables together until tender, about 15 to 20 additional minutes. Drain well. In large bowl, mash with a potato masher or fork until smooth. Beat in milk, butter, salt (if desired), pepper, and nutmeg. Spoon into serving bowl. Sprinkle with chopped parsley. Serve hot. This dish is particularly good with roasted meats.

Rutabagas are born of a turnip and cabbage. This lesser known root vegetable can be cooked in the same ways we cook white potatoes, sweet potatoes, or turnips and combines well with each of them. In this recipe the ratio is half and half; however, each time you make it, play with the proportions to find the balance you prefer. Each year I like to put one new dish on the Thanksgiving table, to create a stir among the old favorites. Count on these underground vegetables to rise to the occasion and add sparkle to your holiday menu.

PER SERVING

CALORIES: **99**
PROTEIN: **2 grams**
FAT: **2 grams**
SODIUM: **39 milligrams**
CHOLESTEROL: **0 milligrams**

Garlic Mashed Potatoes

South American soil was the first to sprout white potatoes. Since that time, new varieties in yellow and purple have been cultivated and widely distributed. I am especially fond of the natural butterlike flavor and color of the Yukon or Finnish Gold potatoes. Count real mashed potatoes among life's simple pleasures. You can't get this kind of comfort and satisfaction from a box.

PER SERVING

CALORIES: **108**
PROTEIN: **4 grams**
FAT: **1 gram**
SODIUM: **71 milligrams**
CHOLESTEROL: **3 milligrams**

◆ 4 SERVINGS

 3 medium-sized potatoes, peeled and quartered
¼ cup skim or 1-percent-fat milk
 1 small garlic clove, minced
 2 tablespoons freshly grated Parmesan cheese
½ teaspoon salt (optional)
¼ teaspoon ground white pepper
Optional garnish: sprinkle of paprika or chopped fresh chives

In 1-quart saucepan, bring 2 cups water to boil; add potatoes. Cover and boil until potatoes are tender when pierced with knife, about 20 minutes. Meanwhile, in small saucepan, combine milk, garlic, cheese, and salt (if desired); heat just until milk is hot and cheese melted. Drain potatoes; over low heat, shake pan for several minutes to dry potatoes well. Press potatoes through sieve, ricer, or food mill into large bowl. Add milk mixture a little at a time, beating after each addition until potatoes are fluffy. Add pepper; garnish with paprika or chives. Serve right away.

Oven "Fried" Okra

◆ 6 SIDE-DISH SERVINGS

1 large egg
½ teaspoon hot pepper sauce
1 pound fresh okra, stem ends trimmed, sliced into ½-inch
   thick rounds
1 cup dry bread crumbs
1 teaspoon freshly ground black pepper
½ teaspoon salt (optional)

1. In large pot ¾ full with salted boiling water, parboil okra until tender, about 5 minutes; drain well.

2. Preheat oven to 450°F. In large bowl, beat together egg, 1 tablespoon water, and pepper sauce; add okra to bowl.

3. In plastic food storage bag, brown paper bag, or large bowl, combine bread crumbs, pepper, and (if desired) salt. Using slotted spoon, remove okra from egg mixture, allowing excess egg mixture to drip back into bowl. Add okra to crumb mixture in bag. Rotate bag to coat okra evenly.

4. On nonstick baking sheet or large shallow pan, spread okra in single layer. Spray okra with nonstick cooking spray. Bake until crisp and golden brown, about 12 minutes. Makes 6 side-dish servings.

These crispy nuggets can be a dream come true for okra lovers. They make tasty cocktail party nibbles and a great change-of-pace side dish. Serve them instead of French fries with burgers. When buying okra, select small to medium-size pods; the larger, more mature pods are not as tender.

PER SERVING
CALORIES: **119**
PROTEIN: **5 grams**
FAT: **2 grams**
SODIUM: **171 milligrams**
CHOLESTEROL: **36 milligrams**

Pícníc Potato Salad

This recipe proves we don't have to give up our favorite dishes to eat healthfully. It's still creamy, but what you taste is potato, not a lot of mayo. Fresh dill adds a mildly distinct flavor and perfume. In fact, you may like the taste of this salad even more than the old style.

PER SERVING

CALORIES: **180**
PROTEIN: **3 grams**
FAT: **7 grams**
SODIUM: **246 milligrams**
CHOLESTEROL: **1 milligram**

◆ 6 SERVINGS

8 to 12 new potatoes or small red-skinned potatoes
1 teaspoon salt (optional)
2 hard-cooked eggs, chopped (optional)
2 scallions, sliced or chopped
2 stalks celery, chopped fine
¼ cup chopped pickle or pickle relish
½ cup low-fat mayonnaise
½ cup low-fat plain yogurt
1 tablespoon prepared mustard
1 tablespoon chopped fresh dill
¼ teaspoon ground white, black, or cayenne pepper
Lettuce leaves
Optional garnish: fresh dill sprigs

1. Scrub potatoes thoroughly; cut away eyes. Peel potatoes only if desired. In large pot, combine potatoes with enough water to cover and add salt if you like; bring to boil. Cook on high heat until tender, about 20 to 30 minutes (do not overcook); drain. When cool enough to handle, quarter potatoes.

2. While potatoes are still warm, combine them in large bowl with eggs, scallions, celery, and pickle.

3. In small bowl, blend mayonnaise, yogurt, mustard, chopped dill, and pepper. Stir dressing into potato salad. Serve on lettuce leaves; garnish with dill sprigs. Serve chilled or at room temperature.

SALAD DAYS
Salads have come a long way since the iceberg lettuce and tomato days. They've moved from a supporting role at mealtime to center stage as main dish courses. We now improvise with crisp greens, low-calorie vegetables, fruits, grains, seafood, poultry, and/or lean meat. Salads offer an endless variety of flavorful, nutritious options. Unfortunately, all too often we undermine their benefits by adding globs of high-fat dressings.

Turnip Tops and Bottoms

◆ 5 SERVINGS

2 bunches turnip greens with bottoms, or if sold
   separately, 1 pound fresh turnips
2 slices turkey bacon, chopped coarse (optional)
½ teaspoon salt (optional)
½ teaspoon freshly ground black pepper

Remove any large, tough stems. Pick through and discard any
brown or yellow leaves. Wash greens well to remove all sand.
Chop greens. Peel turnips and cut into 1-inch cubes. In large
saucepan over medium-low heat, cook bacon several minutes.
Add 2 cups water; bring to simmer. Add greens, stirring to
wilt and submerge in liquid. Stir in salt and pepper. Simmer
about 15 minutes. Add turnip tops; simmer until vegetables
are tender, about 20 additional minutes.

For all of you city dwellers, farmers' markets or a drive to the countryside to find a farm stand are the next best thing to having a garden of your own. I make the trek most Saturdays. Much of the produce is grown by people who care about the land and have high standards of quality for their niche products. I am thrilled to find turnips with greens still attached, as this helps preserve the freshness. Do not detach tops until it is time to cook. Putting aside my general objection to fabricated foods, I find that turkey bacon bits adds a spark of flavor.

PER SERVING

CALORIES: **25**
PROTEIN: **1 gram**
FAT: **0 grams**
SODIUM: **56 milligrams**
CHOLESTEROL: **0 milligrams**

Moroccan Vegetable Stew

Northern Africa, with its unique cultural flavor, enhanced by close proximity to the Mediterranean trade routes, is home to an exotic mix of food experiences. Reflective of a people who live with the extremes of life in the desert, blends of beans and grains in a vegetable medley is common to the region.

PER SERVING

CALORIES: **311**
PROTEIN: **10 grams**
FAT: **6 grams**
SODIUM: **388 milligrams**
CHOLESTEROL: **0 milligrams**

◆ 6 SERVINGS

2 tablespoons olive oil
1 medium-sized yellow onion, sliced lengthwise
2 garlic cloves, minced
1 cup vegetable broth or chicken broth
2 large ripe tomatoes, chopped (about 2 cups)
1 small bell pepper, seeds and membranes removed, cut into chunks
2 medium-sized zucchini, cut into ¼-inch-thick rounds
2 medium-sized carrots, cut into ¼-inch-thick rounds
15-ounce can garbanzo beans, drained and rinsed
1 tablespoon chopped fresh oregano
½ teaspoon paprika
½ teaspoon salt (optional)
¼ teaspoon ground black pepper
5 cups hot cooked couscous

In large saucepan, heat olive oil; cook onion until soft, about 5 minutes. Add garlic; cook until garlic turns golden, about 3 minutes. Stir in broth. Add tomatoes, bell pepper, zucchini, carrots, garbanzo beans, oregano, paprika, salt, and pepper. Cook just until vegetables are tender, about 8 to 10 minutes. Serve over couscous.

Fresh Field Peas with Whole Okra

◆ 6 SERVINGS

  2 tablespoons olive oil
  1 small yellow onion, chopped
  1 bay leaf
  1 teaspoon salt (optional)
  1 teaspoon freshly ground black pepper
  4 cups shelled fresh field peas or fresh black-eyed peas
  ½ pound fresh okra, left whole, tops trimmed

In large saucepan, heat olive oil; add onion and cook gently 5 minutes. Add about 3 cups water, bay leaf, salt, and pepper; bring to boil. Add peas; simmer 20 minutes. Add whole okra; cook until it is tender but not mushy, about 5 to 10 additional minutes (according to size and age of okra). Remove bay leaf and serve.

Okra seems to invite rejection. Not only are the pods fuzzy, they are mucilaginous (fancy word for slimy). To better enjoy the wonderful garden flavor and benefit from okra's wealth of nutrients, smooth away any fuzz by rubbing with a towel. To keep the slippery juices from escaping, leave the pods whole, barely trimming the stem end and leaving the tip intact. As for field peas, buying them in the pod is the top form. Shelling is excellent work for children. Turn this little task into a hands-on lesson about the nature of real food and the way vegetables grow.

PER SERVING

CALORIES: **90**
PROTEIN: **3 grams**
FAT: **5 grams**
SODIUM: **5 milligrams**
CHOLESTEROL: **0 milligrams**

Fireball Vegetable Chili

This meatless main dish is a mosaic of colors, textures, and tastes. Don't be put off by the long list of ingredients; most of them are simply tossed into the pot together. I once served it at a gathering that included hard-core meat eaters. I was all braced for "Where's the beef?" when one of the men asked for the recipe.

PER SERVING

CALORIES: 254
PROTEIN: 9 grams
FAT: 9 grams
SODIUM: 85 milligrams
CHOLESTEROL: 0 milligrams

◆ 8 SERVINGS

1 cup kidney beans, soaked overnight in water to cover
½ cup bulgur
¼ cup virgin olive oil
1 chopped yellow onion
2 garlic cloves, minced
½ cup chopped celery
½ cup chopped carrots
3 tablespoons chili powder
1 tablespoon ground cumin
½ teaspoon cayenne pepper
1½ tablespoons chopped fresh basil
1¼ tablespoons chopped fresh oregano
1 medium-sized summer squash, cubed
1 medium-sized zucchini, cubed
1 small green bell pepper, seeded and diced
1 small red pepper, seeded and diced
1 cup sliced mushrooms
1 large tomato, cubed
6-ounce can tomato paste
1½ cups vegetable broth
1 teaspoon salt (optional)
½ teaspoon freshly ground black pepper

1. Drain water from soaked beans. Place beans in pot with 4 cups fresh water. Cook for 30 to 45 minutes. Drain beans, reserving water. Bring 1 cup bean cooking liquid to boil (reserve the remainder) and pour over bulgur in bowl. Let rest for 30 minutes.

2. In dutch oven, heat olive oil and sauté onion. Add garlic, celery, and carrots; cook until glazed. Add chili powder, cumin, cayenne, basil, and oregano. Cook over low heat for 3 to 5 minutes. Add squash, zucchini, green and red peppers, and mushrooms. Cook for 2 to 3 minutes. Add soaked bulgur, kidney beans, tomato, and reserved liquid. Cook until vegetables are tender.

3. Combine tomato paste with broth in bowl, then add to vegetable mixture. Continue to cook over low heat until mixture is heated through. Season with salt (if desired) and pepper.

Brazilian Black Beans with Marinated Tomatoes

Black is beautiful. These are my favorite type of dried bean. Black beans, also known as turtle beans, are native to South America and come in a variety of sizes and earthy flavors.

◆ 7 SERVINGS

2 cups dried black beans (turtle beans)
2 large garlic cloves
1 onion, studded with 8 whole cloves
2 onions, chopped
1 large green bell pepper, seeds and membranes removed, chopped

Marinated Tomatoes:

6 tomatoes, chopped
1 bunch scallions, including green tops, chopped
½ small red onion, chopped
1 clove garlic, crushed
3 tablespoons wine vinegar
4 to 5 dashes hot pepper sauce

4 cups cooked brown rice

1. In large bowl or colander, rinse beans thoroughly with cold running water, picking through and discarding damaged beans and any debris. Place beans and 6 cups water in large pot. Add the whole garlic cloves and the clove-studded onion. (Make small hole for each clove in side of onion with toothpick; push stem end into hole.) Cook over low heat about 2 hours.

2. Remove garlic and onion. Add chopped onions and green pepper. Cook 1 additional hour until beans are tender.

3. To make marinated tomatoes, combine chopped tomatoes, scallions, chopped onion, garlic, wine vinegar, and hot sauce. Refrigerate until ready to serve, at least 1 hour. Serve beans over brown rice, with some marinated tomatoes on top.

Black-eyed Pea Salad with Lemon Vinaigrette

◆ 8 SIDE-DISH SERVINGS

4 cups cooked black-eyed peas, drained

2 scallions, including green tops, sliced

1 small green bell pepper, seeds and membranes removed, diced

1 large tomato, seeded and diced

1 rib celery, sliced thin

4 large basil leaves, chopped; or 2 teaspoons dried basil or thyme

Lemon Vinaigrette:

¼ cup olive oil or vegetable oil

¼ cup freshly squeezed lemon juice or cider vinegar

1 large garlic clove, minced

1 teaspoon Dijon-style mustard

½ teaspoon grated lemon zest

½ teaspoon ground black pepper

½ teaspoon hot pepper sauce

½ teaspoon salt (optional)

6 cups torn salad greens

1. In large bowl, combine peas, scallions, bell pepper, tomato, celery, and basil.

2. In small bowl or jar with tight-fitting lid, combine olive or vegetable oil, lemon juice, garlic, mustard, lemon zest, black pepper, pepper sauce, and salt (if desired); shake to blend. Pour dressing over vegetable mixture. Gently toss to coat and mix. Cover and refrigerate at least 2 hours.

3. Arrange bed of salad greens in salad bowl or on plates; add marinated vegetable mixture.

This is my version of down-home pea patch meets gourmet. Mild, nutty-tasting black-eyed peas readily absorb flavor and harmonize with spices and herbs. These peas are a nutritional bonanza—rich in protein, complex carbohydrates, and fiber, with no cholesterol or fat. For the best mix and proportion, cut all vegetables for the salad close to the size of the peas.

PER SERVING

CALORIES: **170**

PROTEIN: **8 grams**

FAT: **8 grams**

SODIUM: **30 milligrams**

CHOLESTEROL: **0 milligrams**

Buttermilk Salad Dressing

Buttermilk lives on in the '90s and into a new millennium. This creamy southern-style dressing enhances your salad's garden-fresh flavor and helps it keep its healthful promise.

◆ 1½ CUPS

¾ cup low-fat buttermilk
1 tablespoon vegetable oil
2 teaspoons minced onion
2 teaspoons minced garlic
½ teaspoon granulated sugar
½ teaspoon salt (optional)

In small glass bowl combine buttermilk, vegetable oil, onion, garlic, sugar, and salt (if desired); mix well. Store in tightly covered container and refrigerate until ready to use.

Ríce and Other Graíns of Truth

It's no secret that African Americans played a key role in early industries that sparked this nation's economic greatness. Nowhere was that involvement more pivotal and poignant than in the flourishing rice fields of South Carolina. Three hundred years of cultivation know-how and the intricate hand labor of abducted Africans led to the development of "Carolina gold"—the rice that became a standard for quality throughout the world. When freedom came and African workers left the rice fields, that rice industry collapsed and never recovered. Today, the well-known Carolina brand actually comes from Texas.

As descendants of Africa and the states of the Gulf Coast rice belt—Arkansas, Louisiana, Mississippi, Missouri, and Texas—we still save a special place for rice on our plates. Sprinkled with a little sugar and eaten as cereal, plain or topped with gravy as a side dish, piled high to make a bed for red beans, cooked with seafood and saffron for dinner, or baked into a creamy pudding for dessert, rice continues to be enjoyed by many of us at least once a day.

The really good news is that this historic staple contains a multitude of nutrients, such as thiamine, riboflavin, iron, calcium, phosphorus, and protein. High in complex carbohydrates but low in calories, a half-cup serving of plain rice contains only 82 calories, a mere trace of fat, and no cholesterol.

But you're not limited to just rice. There's a world of low-fat grains the entire family will love, from grits, cornmeal, and spaghetti to barley, bulgur (cracked wheat), couscous, millet, and quinoa, that will make new and welcome additions to the dinner table.

Basic Brown Rice

◆

Spanish Rice with
Green Chiles

◆

Lemon Rice

◆

Shrimp Fried Rice

◆

Caribbean Coconut-Rice Pilaf

◆

Crawfish Jambalaya

◆

Hip Hoppin' John

◆

Bayou Dirty Rice

◆

Rice Salad with Chicken
and Peanuts

◆

Baked Grits with
Caramelized Onions

◆

Grits and Cheese Soufflés

◆

Southern Spoon Bread

◆

Spicy Couscous

◆

Peanutty Noodles

◆

Baked Mac and Cheese

◆

Potluck Macaroni Salad

◆ Season your rice while it cooks, and skip the gravy. Cooking rice, couscous, and other grains with low-fat, low-sodium broth, scallions or onions, and herbs steeps in flavor. You can avoid the 10 grams of fat and 100 calories in 2 tablespoons of gravy.

◆ Put your juicer to work. Freshly squeezed vegetable juices such as carrot, celery, and cucumber are great for cooking rice and soaking bulgur.

◆ Get to know basmati and other aromatic rices. They have a great built-in flavor, and the taste is similar to roasted popcorn or nuts. Added seasonings are not needed.

◆ For a sweet touch, cook grains in diluted orange juice or apple juice. Stir in curry powder, white pepper, or chili powder; raisins, dates, or toasted almonds.

◆ Lighten up your baked macaroni and cheese. You can keep that golden, cheese-rich taste and lose the fat by switching to nonfat and reduced-fat cheeses. Nonfat cheeses are stiffer than full-fat cheese, so shred them more finely to improve melting.

◆ Play down the "fried" in fried rice. A nonstick skillet or wok and just a teaspoon or two of vegetable, peanut, or sesame oil can provide the familiar "fried" flavor.

◆ If you can't eat your grits without butter, ease up. A tablespoon of butter contains 11 grams of fat and 100 calories. Cut back to a teaspoon and slash those numbers by two-thirds.

Basic Brown Rice

◆ 3 TO 4 CUPS; 7 SERVINGS

1 cup uncooked brown rice
2 to 2½ cups liquid (water, broth, juice)
½ teaspoon salt (optional)

1. In 2- to 3-quart saucepan, combine ingredients. Bring to boil; stir once or twice.

2. Reduce heat, cover, and simmer until rice is tender and liquid is absorbed, about 45 to 50 minutes. Fluff with fork.

Brown rice has nothing added, nothing taken away. It is one of nature's most healthful foods. Its nuttiness gives it more flavor than white rice, yet many folks, because they're not sure how to cook it, opt for its less nutritious, refined counterpart. It does take longer to cook, so prepare a double batch and keep the extra on hand for up to a week for quick use in casseroles, soup, and salads. If package directions are not available, follow this easy method.

PER ¹/₂ CUP SERVING

CALORIES: 98
PROTEIN: 2 grams
FAT: 1 gram
SODIUM: 2 milligrams
CHOLESTEROL: 0 milligrams

Spanish Rice with Green Chiles

Tomato-flavored and spicy, this rice pilaf makes a tasty side dish. Turn it into a main course by adding cooked meat, poultry, fish, or vegetables before the rice is covered to steam.

PER SERVING

CALORIES: **142**
PROTEIN: **3 grams**
FAT: **3 grams**
SODIUM: **254 milligrams**
CHOLESTEROL: **0 milligrams**

◆ 4 SERVINGS

2 teaspoons vegetable oil
1 small yellow onion, chopped fine
2 cloves garlic, minced
½ cup uncooked long-grain white rice
1 teaspoon chili powder
14½-ounce can tomatoes, chopped (reserve juice)
3-ounce can green chiles, chopped
1 bay leaf
¼ teaspoon salt (optional)
¼ teaspoon ground black pepper

1. In heavy 3-quart saucepan, heat vegetable oil; sauté onion, garlic, and rice until rice is lightly browned. Stir in chili powder, tomatoes and juice, green chiles, ½ cup water, bay leaf, salt (if desired), and pepper. Bring to boil; lower heat to simmer.

2. Cover and cook until rice is tender, about 20 minutes. For drier rice, uncover and cook 5 additional minutes. Remove and discard bay leaf. Serve warm.

Lemon Rice

◆ 8 SERVINGS

  1 tablespoon margarine

  1 tablespoon chopped fresh dill, thyme, or mint, or
    1 teaspoon dried herb

  1 tablespoon fresh lemon juice

  1 teaspoon grated lemon zest

1½ cups uncooked long-grain rice

  3 cups All-purpose Vegetable Broth (page 18) or water,
    heated

 ½ teaspoon salt (optional)

 ¼ teaspoon white pepper

1. In heavy 3-quart saucepan with lid, melt margarine over medium-high heat. Add herb of choice, lemon juice, and zest; cook 2 minutes. Stir in rice until coated; cook and stir about 2 minutes. Add heated broth and salt (if desired) to rice mixture, stirring constantly.

2. Lower heat, cover, and simmer until rice is tender and all liquid is absorbed, about 18 minutes. Season with pepper; fluff with fork. Serve immediately.

The subtle zing of citrus adds surprising appeal to the familiar grain. This side dish makes a perfect pairing with fish, seafood, or chicken.

PER SERVING

CALORIES: **153**
PROTEIN: **3 grams**
FAT: **2 grams**
SODIUM: **49 milligrams**
CHOLESTEROL: **0 milligrams**

Shrimp Fried Rice

Our most popular choice for Chinese take-out, this well-seasoned stir-fry is easy to make at home. You'll find this version far less greasy and much fresher in taste. Keep cooked rice on hand, tightly covered in the fridge for up to five days, as a shortcut to making quick weekday meals.

◆ 4 SERVINGS

¼ cup Basic Chicken Broth (page 19) or low-sodium canned broth
2 tablespoons reduced-sodium soy sauce
½ teaspoon sugar
⅛ teaspoon ground black pepper
⅛ teaspoon cayenne pepper
2 tablespoons peanut oil or vegetable oil
3 cups cold cooked rice
1 cup cooked small shrimp
1 cup fresh bean sprouts
½ cup cooked fresh green peas
½ cup seeded, chopped yellow bell pepper
2 scallions, including green tops, sliced thin

1. In small bowl, blend broth, soy sauce, sugar, and black and cayenne pepper; set aside.

2. In large heavy skillet or wok, heat peanut or vegetable oil over medium heat. Add rice and stir quickly until golden, pressing out any lumps.

3. Add shrimp, bean sprouts, green peas, bell pepper, and scallions; stir-fry for 2 minutes. Stir in soy sauce mixture; cover and cook 1 minute. Serve hot.

Caribbean Coconut-Rice Pilaf

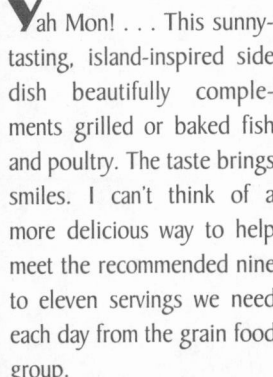

 6 SERVINGS

    2 teaspoons butter or margarine
    1 scallion, including green top, sliced thin
 1½ cups uncooked long-grain white rice
    1 medium-sized carrot, shredded
  ⅓ cup golden raisins
  ¼ cup unsweetened shredded coconut
  ¾ cup canned coconut milk
    2 cups All-purpose Vegetable Broth (page 18), Basic
      Chicken Broth (page 19), or low-sodium canned broth or
      water
  ¼ teaspoon ground white pepper

1. In heavy saucepan over medium heat, melt butter. Add scallion; cook and stir about 5 minutes. Stir in rice, carrot, raisins, and half of shredded coconut. Cook and stir until rice starts to turn translucent.

2. Stir in coconut milk, broth, and pepper. Bring to boil; reduce heat to low. Cover and simmer 20 minutes. Remove from heat; set aside, still covered, 10 minutes.

3. Meanwhile, preheat oven to 350°F. Spread remaining coconut on baking sheet. Toast just until light golden brown, about 5 minutes. Sprinkle toasted coconut over top of rice.

Yah Mon! . . . This sunny-tasting, island-inspired side dish beautifully complements grilled or baked fish and poultry. The taste brings smiles. I can't think of a more delicious way to help meet the recommended nine to eleven servings we need each day from the grain food group.

PER SERVING

CALORIES: **305**
PROTEIN: **5 grams**
FAT: **10 grams**
SODIUM: **53 milligrams**
CHOLESTEROL: **3 milligrams**

Crawfish Jambalaya

Jambalaya is a Creole rice classic. One explanation of its roots says that the name comes from JAMON, the Spanish word for ham, the meat that studs authentic versions of the dish. This recipe calls for turkey ham, but if you prefer, lean pork ham can certainly be used. I also add tomatoes (that's the way my mother made it), although in my research I found jambalaya recipes sans tomatoes by master Creole chefs. Take your pick and make it the way you like it; that's what jambalaya is all about.

PER SERVING

CALORIES: **230**
PROTEIN: **21 grams**
FAT: **3 grams**
SODIUM: **562 milligrams**
CHOLESTEROL: **100 milligrams**

◆ 6 SERVINGS

Nonstick cooking spray
½-pound piece turkey ham, diced into small pieces
  1 medium-sized yellow onion, chopped
  1 small green bell pepper, seeds and membranes removed, chopped
  1 rib celery, sliced thin
  1 garlic clove, minced
  1 tablespoon chopped fresh parsley
  1 cup uncooked long-grain white rice
  1 pound blanched crawfish tails, with their fat (available seasonally at southern and full-service fish markets), or small shrimp
 ½ cup chopped peeled fresh tomatoes
  2 cups Basic Chicken Broth (page 19), low-sodium canned broth, or water
  1 tablespoon chopped thyme leaves or 1 teaspoon dried thyme
  1 teaspoon hot pepper sauce
 ½ teaspoon salt (optional)
 ½ teaspoon paprika
 ¼ teaspoon freshly ground black pepper
  1 bay leaf

1. In dutch oven coated with nonstick cooking spray, combine ham, onion, bell pepper, celery, garlic, and parsley. Over low heat, cover and cook gently until vegetables are tender, about 8 minutes (stir occasionally, and add small amount of broth if needed to prevent sticking).

2. Add rice; stir to mix well. Add crawfish tails, tomatoes, broth, thyme, hot pepper sauce, salt, paprika, pepper, and bay leaf. Bring to low boil; cook about 3 minutes. Reduce heat to low. Cover and simmer, stirring occasionally to facilitate even cooking, until rice is tender, about 35 minutes. Using fork, fluff jambalaya. Discard bay leaf. Serve warm with crusty French bread.

Hip Hoppin' John

◆ 6 SIDE-DISH OR 4 MAIN-DISH SERVINGS

1 cup dried black-eyed peas
1 tablespoon vegetable oil
1 medium-sized yellow onion, chopped
1 garlic clove, minced
1 cup uncooked long-grain regular or converted white rice
1 teaspoon crushed hot red pepper flakes
1 small red or green bell pepper, seeds and membranes removed, chopped
1 bay leaf
1 tablespoon chopped fresh thyme or 1 teaspoon dried thyme
1 teaspoon salt (optional)
½ teaspoon freshly ground black pepper

Although the Old South gets the credit for creating this black-eyed-peas-and-rice-theme dish, there are national variations throughout the Caribbean and Africa.

PER EACH OF **6** SERVINGS
CALORIES: **209**
PROTEIN: **7 grams**
FAT: **3 grams**
SODIUM: **6 milligrams**
CHOLESTEROL: **0 milligrams**

1. Place peas in colander; rinse thoroughly with cold running water, picking through and discarding shriveled, broken, or discolored peas and any debris. In large bowl or dutch oven, cover peas with about 1 quart water; soak overnight. Drain peas and discard water; transfer peas to colander and rinse with cold running water.

2. In dutch oven or kettle, cover soaked peas with 5 cups fresh water. Bring liquid to boil; reduce heat to low. Simmer peas until tender yet still firm, about 40 minutes.

3. Meanwhile, in large skillet, heat vegetable oil; sauté onion and garlic just until golden, about 5 minutes. Use your judgment or measuring cup to make sure liquid remaining in peas equals about 2½ cups; if not, supplement with water or broth. Add sautéed onion mixture and remaining ingredients to pot with peas; stir to mix well. Cover tightly; cook over low heat until rice and peas are tender, about 15 minutes. Discard bay leaf.

Bayou Dirty Rice

The specks of chicken liver and gizzard can be blamed for this less-than-appetizing name. The credit for the terrific flavor goes to the harmonious and highly complementary mix of ingredients. You may want to increase the serving size and enjoy this dish as a main course. Serve with kale or other deep green vegetable.

PER EACH OF **6** SERVINGS

CALORIES: **257**
PROTEIN: **13 grams**
FAT: **4 grams**
SODIUM: **43 milligrams**
CHOLESTEROL: **169 milligrams**

◆ 6 SIDE-DISH OR 4 MAIN-DISH SERVINGS

1½ cups uncooked long-grain white rice
 1 tablespoon vegetable oil
 1 medium-sized onion, chopped fine
 1 garlic clove, minced
 ½ pound chicken livers, chopped fine
 4 ounces chicken gizzards, chopped fine
 2 scallions, green tops included, chopped fine
 2 stalks celery, including leafy parts, chopped fine
 ¼ cup minced green bell pepper
 1 sprig parsley, minced
 ¼ teaspoon salt (optional)
 ¼ teaspoon ground black pepper

1. Cook rice according to directions on page 73, until almost done, about 15 minutes. Drain well and set aside.

2. In heavy skillet, heat vegetable oil and sauté onion and garlic. Add chopped chicken livers and gizzards to onion and garlic mixture and sauté until cooked and crumbly, about 4 minutes.

3. Add scallions, celery, green pepper, parsley, salt, pepper, and drained rice; continue to cook over medium heat until rice is thoroughly cooked. Toss gently until ingredients are well mixed; serve at once.

Rice Salad with Chicken and Peanuts

◆ 4 SERVINGS

2 teaspoons salt (optional; much will be discarded with cooking water)

¾ cup uncooked long-grain white rice or converted rice

2 tablespoons vegetable oil

2 tablespoons reduced-sodium chicken broth

¼ cup red wine vinegar or fresh lemon juice

¼ teaspoon ground black pepper

3 cups cubed cooked chicken breasts

⅓ cup roasted unsalted peanuts

1 rib celery, sliced thin

1 large scallion, sliced thin

¼ cup chopped flat-leaf parsley

3 tablespoons drained small capers

Lettuce leaves (optional)

1. In large pot, bring 3 quarts water to boil; stir in salt (if desired). Add rice; cook uncovered over medium-high heat until tender, about 15 minutes. Drain in colander, rinse with cold water; drain again. Place rice in large bowl.

2. In small bowl, mix vegetable oil, broth, vinegar or lemon juice, and black pepper; drizzle dressing over rice. Add cubed chicken, peanuts, celery, scallion, parsley, and capers; toss to mix and coat.

3. Line platter or salad bowl with lettuce; add rice salad.

Cooking rice in lots of boiling water (the way we cook pasta) eliminates the worry of getting the amount of water right. White rice is ready in 15 to 18 minutes; brown rice will be done in 35 to 40 minutes.

PER SERVING

CALORIES: **364**
PROTEIN: **32 grams**
FAT: **16 grams**
SODIUM: **409 milligrams**
CHOLESTEROL: **34 milligrams**

Baked Grits with Caramelized Onions

When heat draws the natural sugar from onions and the sugar is cooked until browned, the resulting caramel flavor is sensational. Look for Vidalia (from Georgia), Oso Sweet, and other brands of sweet onions that appear in late spring and early summer.

PER SERVING

CALORIES: **221**
PROTEIN: **9 grams**
FAT: **10 grams**
SODIUM: **138 milligrams**
CHOLESTEROL: **30 milligrams**

◆ 6 SERVINGS

Nonstick cooking spray or butter
 1 teaspoon salt (optional)
 1 cup stone-ground grits
 2 tablespoons butter or margarine
 1 medium-sized yellow onion, sliced crosswise into thin rings
 2 egg whites, lightly beaten
 1 teaspoon paprika
 ¼ to ½ teaspoon hot pepper sauce

1. Preheat oven to 350°F. Coat 2-quart baking dish or soufflé dish with nonstick cooking spray or mere smear of butter; set aside.

2. In large saucepan (grits expand considerably in volume while cooking), bring 4 cups of water to boil. Sprinkle in salt (if desired) and grits, a portion at a time, stirring constantly. Reduce heat to low simmer. Cook, stirring occasionally from bottom to prevent sticking, until grits are thick and soft in texture, about 15 minutes.

3. While grits are cooking, melt 1 tablespoon butter in non-stick skillet over low heat; add onion. Slowly cook and stir until onion is uniformly browned but not burned, about 10 minutes. (Do not hurry.) Add small amount of water if needed to avoid sticking.

4. Remove grits from heat. Stir in caramelized onion, remaining 1 tablespoon butter, egg whites, paprika, and hot sauce. Pour grits mixture into prepared baking dish. Bake until grits are lightly firm and knife inserted in center comes out clean, about 50 minutes. Serve right away.

Gríts and Cheese Soufflés

◆ 6 SERVINGS

Nonstick cooking spray

 1 cup white or yellow grits

½ teaspoon salt (optional)

 2 scallions, including green tops, chopped fine

 2 garlic cloves, minced

 1 tablespoon chopped fresh thyme

 1 cup (4 ounces) shredded reduced-fat Cheddar cheese

 1 egg yolk

¼ teaspoon cayenne pepper

 3 egg whites

1. Preheat oven to 400°F. Coat six 8-ounce soufflé dishes with nonstick cooking spray; set aside.

2. In saucepan, bring 4 cups water, grits, and (if desired) salt to boil. Cook and stir until thickened; remove from heat. Beat in scallions, garlic, thyme, cheese, egg yolk, and pepper.

3. In clean, deep bowl, beat egg whites until stiff but not dry. Fold into grits mixture. Pour into prepared soufflé dishes. Bake until puffed and browned, about 25 minutes.

While grits are about as down-home as you can get, soufflés are regarded as high falutin. The combination of the two in these individually baked servings makes a particularly scrumptious course for a dinner party or luncheon.

PER SERVING

CALORIES: 170
PROTEIN: 10 grams
FAT: 4 grams
SODIUM: 122 milligrams
CHOLESTEROL: 49 milligrams

Southern Spoon Bread

Once you sample this custardlike cornmeal pudding, you'll understand why it became a staple of southern cooking. Serve in place of rice, potatoes, or dressing (which it resembles).

◆ 6 SERVINGS

Nonstick cooking spray
2 teaspoons butter
½ cup finely chopped yellow onion or scallions
1 cup white or yellow cornmeal
2 teaspoons sugar
2 teaspoons baking powder
½ teaspoon salt (optional)
3 cups 1-percent-fat milk
1 egg yolk
3 egg whites

1. Preheat oven to 350°F. Coat 1½-quart baking dish or soufflé dish with nonstick cooking spray; set aside. Heat butter in nonstick skillet; sauté onion until tender, about 5 minutes.

2. In small bowl, combine cornmeal, sugar, baking powder, salt (if desired), and 1 cup milk; stir until blended. In 3-quart saucepan over medium heat, scald remaining 2 cups milk (heat just until tiny bubbles form around edges of pan). Stir in cornmeal mixture; cook, stirring occasionally, until mixture resembles thick mush, 4 to 5 minutes. Remove from heat; let cool slightly.

3. In medium-sized bowl, beat egg yolk slightly; stir in a little of cornmeal mixture. Stir yolk into warm cornmeal; mix well. Using rubber spatula to scrape skillet, stir in onion mixture.

4. In small, clean, deep bowl, beat egg whites until stiff. Fold ⅓ of whites into cornmeal mixture to lighten; fold in remaining egg whites until evenly blended. Spoon batter into prepared dish. Bake until puffed and golden brown, about 30 to 40 minutes. Spoon onto plates to serve.

Spicy Couscous

◆ 8 SERVINGS

1 tablespoon butter or margarine

1 medium-sized yellow onion, chopped fine

2 garlic cloves, minced

2 teaspoons curry powder, or to taste

⅛ teaspoon black pepper

½ teaspoon crushed red pepper flakes

3 cups All-purpose Vegetable Broth (page 18), Basic Chicken Broth (page 19), or low-sodium canned broth

2 cups uncooked quick couscous

1. In 5-quart saucepan or dutch oven, heat butter. Add onion; sauté about 5 minutes. Add garlic; cook until onion begins to brown around the edges, about 3 additional minutes.

2. Stir in curry powder, pepper, and pepper flakes, then broth; mix well. Bring mixture to boil; gradually add couscous, stirring briskly to prevent lumping.

3. Cover and remove from heat; let stand undisturbed until all liquid is absorbed and no raw taste remains, about 6 minutes. Fluff with fork to separate grains.

Couscous is the Arabic word for granular semolina (ground durum wheat). It is also the name of the North African stew served over it. To you, it can mean a warm side dish that is delicious, goes well with just about everything, and is incredibly easy to make.

PER SERVING

CALORIES: **208**

PROTEIN: **7 grams**

FAT: **2 grams**

SODIUM: **51 milligrams**

CHOLESTEROL: **4 milligrams**

Peanutty Noodles

"**D**own home" in this case may be southern China. I'm not sure of this recipe's origin; I only know it's a really good-tasting side dish that can be turned into a main dish by adding steamed vegetables, chicken, or shrimp.

PER SERVING

CALORIES: **223**
PROTEIN: **9 grams**
FAT: **10 grams**
SODIUM: **269 milligrams**
CHOLESTEROL: **42 milligrams**

◆ 6 SERVINGS

8 ounces uncooked linguine
1 cup reduced-sodium chicken broth
2 tablespoons reduced-sodium soy sauce
2 tablespoons cider vinegar
1 tablespoon packed brown sugar
2 teaspoons grated fresh ginger or 1 teaspoon ground ginger
1 teaspoon roasted sesame oil
2 garlic cloves, minced
½ teaspoon crushed red pepper
⅓ cup creamy peanut butter
Optional garnishes: diagonally sliced scallions (including green tops), julienned cucumber

1. Cook linguine according to package directions.

2. Meanwhile, in large skillet combine broth, soy sauce, vinegar, brown sugar, ginger, sesame oil, garlic, and red pepper. Over medium heat, bring to boil, stirring frequently.

3. Using wire whisk, stir in peanut butter until smooth. Reduce heat and simmer until slightly thickened, about 2 minutes. Remove from heat.

4. Drain linguine; toss with peanut sauce. Serve warm, at room temperature, or chilled; sprinkle with scallions or cucumber if you like.

Baked Mac and Cheese

◆ 4 SERVINGS

8 ounces uncooked elbow macaroni
2 tablespoons light butter or margarine
1 scallion, thinly sliced
2 tablespoons unbleached all-purpose flour
¼ teaspoon dry mustard
½ teaspoon hot pepper sauce
½ teaspoon salt (optional)
2 cups skim milk
1 cup (4 ounces) shredded fat-reduced sharp cheddar cheese
Nonstick cooking spray
Paprika

1. Heat oven to 350°F. Cook macaroni according to package directions.

2. Meanwhile, in medium-sized saucepan over medium heat, melt butter; sauté scallion until tender, about 5 minutes. Into butter mixture, blend flour, dry mustard, pepper sauce (if desired), salt; cook and stir constantly, 1 minute.

3. Gradually stir in milk; cook and stir until thickened, about 10 minutes. Remove from heat; stir in cheese until melted.

4. Drain macaroni well; stir into cheese mixture. Spoon macaroni mixture into 1½-quart baking dish coated with cooking spray; sprinkle with paprika.

5. Bake until set, about 25 minutes.

I would be hard-pressed to find the culinary roots of this hallmark of soulful cooking. I have no idea as to when or where it first appeared, only that it shows up for EVERY special occasion and many everyday meals.

PER SERVING

CALORIES: **192**
PROTEIN: **10 grams**
FAT: **4 grams**
SODIUM: **233 milligrams**
CHOLESTEROL: **8 milligrams**

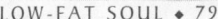

Potluck Macaroni Salad

This classic salad makes a wonderful buffet dish for a summer barbecue. For the sake of good taste, don't overdress it! Prepare this salad early in the day and slip it into the fridge to cool the pasta and meld the flavors.

PER SERVING

CALORIES: **254**
PROTEIN: **9 grams**
FAT: **11 grams**
SODIUM: **183 milligrams**
CHOLESTEROL: **20 milligrams**

◆ 8 SERVINGS

8 ounces uncooked small elbow macaroni (4 cups cooked)
1 cup low-fat mayonnaise
2 tablespoons cider vinegar
1 teaspoon granulated sugar
2 teaspoons prepared mustard
½ teaspoon salt (optional)
⅛ teaspoon ground black pepper
1 cup (4 ounces) diced reduced-fat Cheddar cheese (optional)
1 cup cooked green peas
1 cup sliced or diced celery
½ cup sliced scallions, including green tops
½ cup sliced radishes
¼ cup chopped sweet pickle

1. Cook macaroni according to package directions; drain. Pour cold water over macaroni; let stand while preparing salad.

2. In small bowl, combine mayonnaise, vinegar, sugar, mustard, salt (if desired), and pepper. Drain cooked macaroni well.

3. In large salad bowl, combine macaroni, cheese, peas, celery, scallions, pickle, and radishes. Pour mayonnaise mixture over macaroni mixture; toss to blend. Serve immediately, or cover and refrigerate until ready to serve.

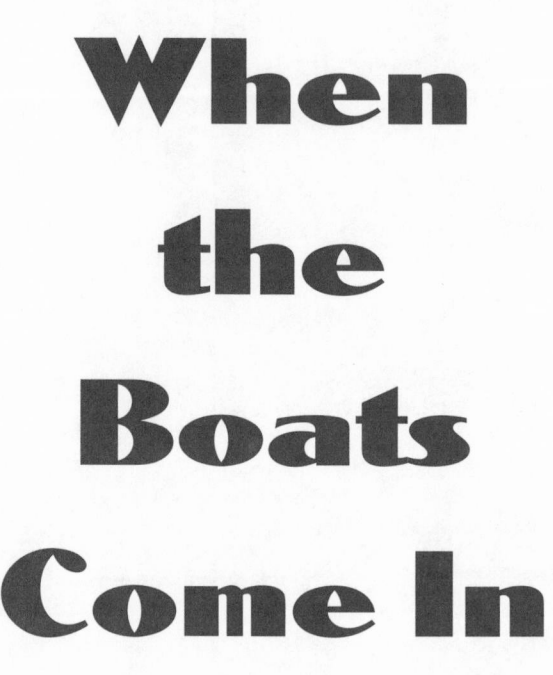

When the Boats Come In

Life mirrors scenes from old, faded postcards in quaint fishing villages that still dot the shores of many Caribbean islands. In Rocky Point, on the coast of the parish of Clarendon in Jamaica, fishermen with deeply burnished skin and sun-bleached hair still hand-carve their boats from cotton-tree logs. They set off to work about two o'clock each morning and are far out to sea when the sun rises and the fish begin to feed. By noon, customers, tourists, and higglers (vendors) have gathered at the shore for first pick of the day's catch. Some higglers rush the fresh fish to their stalls at the open market, others peddle door to door, and still other entrepreneurial souls fry the fish and sell it with bammi (casava cakes) right on the shore. The village takes on color and comes alive.

In New York City a similar scenario unfolds each day at the vast Fulton Fish Market. Chefs from trendy restaurants, seafood purveyors, and home cooks begin to gather at five o'clock in the morning for an early pick of the bounty from the big boats.

As fresh fish is highly perishable, use your good senses no matter where you shop. Take a close look—fillets and steaks should appear moist, firm, and freshly cut; whole fish should have glistening skin and red or bright pink gills. Give a sniff—good quality fish smells sea-fresh; avoid any that has a strong or "fishy" odor. Press the flesh—it should spring back and not leave an indentation when touched.

Be adventurous when you shop for seafood—there's a sea of tasty choices. Some fish are almost fat-free, while others are moderately fatty, yet all are considered healthful because of their Omega-3 fatty acids. Scientists are still unraveling the exact role of these acids known to be a boon for the blood— reducing its cholesterol, lowering pressure, and preventing heart attacks and strokes caused by clots. Monkfish, orange roughy, rockfish, skate, sea bass, mussels, and scallops are excellent choices for a change of course. Or try tilapia—a sweet-tasting, lean fish from Africa that is now being raised on aquaculture farms here in the States. (Some biblical scholars believe tilapia to be the fish with which Jesus fed the multitude.)

And did I mention that fish dishes are excellent for parties? When you're having a hard time keeping track of who eats meat and who has given it up, fish becomes a good choice for pleasing nearly everyone.

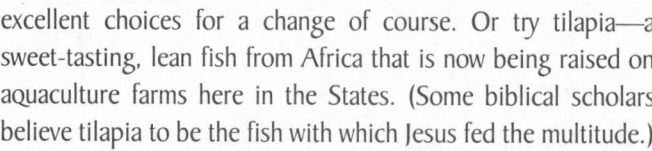

Fat Chat

Seafood is naturally low in fat and cholesterol. Some feel that fish nourishes the brain. Regardless, consider it smart food.

◆ Don't reach for the frying pan. Take out the fish poacher, bamboo steamer basket, broiler rack, or roasting pan. These pieces of equipment cook fish easily and deliciously with no added fat.

◆ Fire up the grill. Fin fish and shellfish are both good choices for grilling. Toss a handful of mesquite or sprigs of fresh herbs on the fire for even more exquisite flavor.

◆ Try your hand at en papillote. The name comes from the French word for COCOON. In this cooking method, fish is wrapped, along with vegetables and seasoning, in parchment paper, then baked. For a simplified version, wrap and bake in a sheet of aluminum foil.

◆ Rub it in. A mixture of dry seasonings rubbed onto fish, then refrigerated to marinate, produces layers of flavor.

◆ Select water-packed canned tuna. A 3½-ounce can of light tuna packed in oil, then drained, contains 200 calories, compared with 130 calories for water-packed. When only oil-packed canned fish is available, drain it well, sprinkle with diluted lemon juice, then drain again for removal of more oil.

Friday Night Catfish (Oven-Fried) with Tangy Tartar Sauce

◆ 8 SERVINGS

Tangy Tartar Sauce:

 1 cup plain low-fat yogurt
 2 tablespoons minced sweet pickles
 2 tablespoons minced capers
 ½ teaspoon minced fresh tarragon
 ½ teaspoon dry mustard
 1 teaspoon salt (optional)
 ½ teaspoon ground white pepper

 ½ cup unbleached all-purpose flour
 1 teaspoon salt (optional)
 1 teaspoon freshly ground black pepper
 1 egg white
 1 teaspoon hot sauce
 ½ cup buttermilk
 4 cups corn bread crumbs
 8 catfish fillets, 5 ounces each

1. In small bowl, combine all tartar sauce ingredients; stir to mix well. Cover and store in refrigerator overnight. Makes about 1 cup.

2. Preheat oven to 450°F. On piece of waxed paper, mix flour, salt (if desired), and pepper. In small bowl, beat egg white, hot sauce, and buttermilk together. On another piece of waxed paper, place corn bread crumbs. Coat each fillet lightly with flour mixture and shake off excess. Dip floured fillets into milk mixture and allow excess to drip back into bowl. Press wet fillets into bread crumbs firmly, coating on both sides.

Throughout the American South, the "fish fry" is as hallowed a culinary tradition as you can find. Concern about fat is no longer a reason to bypass this gastronomical treat. Oven "frying" is a healthy substitute for deep-fat frying. If you don't overcook the fish, the outside will be crisp and crunchy while the inside stays moist and flavorful. You can serve this tasty fish with anything you choose, as long as it's coleslaw and hush puppies. (Note that the tartar sauce is best when prepared a day ahead.)

PER SERVING WITHOUT SAUCE

CALORIES: **345**
PROTEIN: **28 grams**
FAT: **15 grams**
SODIUM: **465 milligrams**
CHOLESTEROL: **86 milligrams**

SAUCE, PER TABLESPOON

CALORIES: **26**
PROTEIN: **2 grams**
FAT: **1 gram**
SODIUM: **143 milligrams**
CHOLESTEROL: **2 milligrams**

3. Place footed grid or cake rack large enough to hold fillets on baking sheet. Arrange coated fillets fairly close together on rack and put in oven. Bake for 10 to 15 minutes, or until fish flakes when tested with a fork. Serve with Tangy Tartar Sauce.

Catfish Florentine

◆ 4 SERVINGS

1 pound fresh spinach
Nonstick cooking spray
1 cup finely chopped onions
1 cup finely chopped celery
1/4 cup finely chopped red bell pepper
1 garlic clove, minced
1/2 teaspoon salt (optional)
1/2 teaspoon ground white pepper
1/2 teaspoon ground thyme
1/2 teaspoon paprika
1/4 teaspoon cayenne pepper
4 catfish fillets (about 5 ounces each) or any firm, white-fleshed fish
1/3 cup shredded reduced-fat Swiss-style cheese

1. Preheat oven to 375°F. Rinse spinach under cold water, remove stems, and set aside. Coat medium-sized skillet with nonstick cooking spray; place over high heat. Add onions, celery, bell pepper, and garlic; sauté 5 minutes. Add spinach leaves and cook, stirring, 5 minutes longer. Remove from heat and set aside.

2. In small bowl, combine salt (if desired), white pepper, thyme, paprika, and ground red pepper. Mix well and sprinkle on both sides of fish. Spread 2 tablespoons of spinach mixture across middle of each fillet, then roll up, jelly-roll fashion. Spoon remaining spinach mixture into 9-inch-square baking dish. Add fish fillets. Cover with aluminum foil; bake 25 minutes. Uncover, sprinkle with cheese, and bake until fish flakes easily with fork and cheese is melted, about 5 additional minutes.

Catfish has cleaned up its act and is now farm-raised and appearing on menus in some fancy digs. The mild sweet taste of catfish goes so well with other foods. It's superb with spinach in these fish roll-ups.

PER SERVING

CALORIES: **215**
PROTEIN: **31 grams**
FAT: **6 grams**
SODIUM: **119 milligrams**
CHOLESTEROL: **88 milligrams**

Catch-of-the-Day Stew

"Easy does it" when making a fish stew. Most fish disintegrate quickly when simmered, and most shellfish toughen; so keep the simmer low and gentle. This savory dish is a showpiece; serve it in a lovely tureen. Have lots of crusty bread on hand.

PER SERVING

CALORIES: **234**
PROTEIN: **26 grams**
FAT: **6 grams**
SODIUM: **354 milligrams**
CHOLESTEROL: **83 milligrams**

◆ 8 SERVINGS

2 tablespoons olive oil
1 large yellow onion, chopped fine
1 celery rib, sliced thin
2 garlic cloves, minced
Two 8-ounce bottles clam juice
4 cups puréed tomatoes
1 dozen raw mussels (fresh mussel shells should either be tightly closed or close when tapped)
2 small zucchini, cut into ½-inch slices
2 ears husked corn, cut into 2-inch pieces
½ teaspoon salt (optional)
¼ teaspoon ground black pepper
¼ teaspoon hot pepper sauce
1 tablespoon chopped fresh chives or 1 teaspoon dried chives
1 tablespoon chopped fresh basil or 1 teaspoon dried basil
1 large bay leaf
1 pound fish fillets, cut into 1-inch cubes (white bass, cod, and monkfish are sturdy, lean choices)
½ pound sea scallops, halved
½ pound medium shrimp (tails on), shelled and deveined
2 tablespoons chopped fresh parsley

1. In 6-quart stockpot or dutch oven, heat olive oil; add onion, celery, and garlic. Sauté until tender, about 5 minutes. Stir in clam juice and tomatoes; gently simmer 15 minutes.

2. Meanwhile, scrub mussels; scrape off any loose barnacles; cut off beards. Steam mussels until they open in large saucepan with about 1 inch water, about 4 to 5 minutes; discard any unopened shells. Set aside.

3. Add zucchini, corn, salt (if desired), black pepper, hot pepper sauce, and herbs, except parsley, to stockpot; simmer about 8 minutes. Add fish, scallops, shrimp, and parsley; simmer until all fish is cooked, about 3 to 5 additional minutes. Discard bay leaf. Add mussels; cook through just until heated. Transfer to tureen or individual bowls.

Baked Stuffed Red Snapper

The natural beauty of a whole snapper and its mild, meaty flavor make this an impressive dish. Guests will think you put in far more effort than you actually did. One holiday season when I was a semi-vegetarian (a vegetarian most of the time, but occasionally I ate fish), I served this snapper dish for Thanksgiving. My menu featured all the trimmings—baked acorn squash, mashed turnips, braised kale, glazed yams, and more. The meal was so festive that no one squawked about the absence of turkey.

PER SERVING

CALORIES: **213**
PROTEIN: **30 grams**
FAT: **5 grams**
SODIUM: **177 milligrams**
CHOLESTEROL: **55 milligrams**

◆ 6 SERVINGS

4-pound whole red snapper, dressed
  1 teaspoon salt (optional)
  1 tablespoon chopped fresh thyme or 1 teaspoon dried
  2 tablespoons fresh lemon juice
  1 teaspoon vegetable oil
  1 tablespoon butter
¾ cup minced celery
½ cup chopped onion
  3 cups day-old bread cubes
  1 teaspoon poultry seasoning
½ teaspoon freshly ground black pepper
½ cup vegetable broth, clam juice, or water
Optional garnishes: celery leaves, dill sprigs, flat-leaf parsley sprigs, lemon and/or lime wedges

1. Rinse fish with cold running water; blot dry with paper towels. Sprinkle fish inside and outside with salt (if desired), thyme, and lemon juice; brush with vegetable oil. Cover and let rest while preparing stuffing.

2. Preheat oven to 350°F. In nonstick skillet, heat butter over medium-low heat. Add celery and onion; cook and stir about 5 minutes.

3. In large bowl, combine bread cubes, sautéed celery and onion, poultry seasoning, black pepper, and liquid; stir until mixed. Using large spoon, lightly fill fish cavity with stuffing mixture. Skewer cavity closed with wooden picks. Brush fish with oil.

4. Place fish in lightly oiled large shallow roasting pan. Bake until fish is cooked through and flesh flakes when tested with knife, about 1 hour. Use 2 wide spatulas or pancake turners to remove fish from pan and transfer to warm platter. Remove picks and garnish.

Fish Dinner Baked in Foil

◆ 4 SERVINGS

4 firm-textured fish fillets or steaks, such as catfish, cod, halibut, tile, monkfish, or tilapia
½ teaspoon salt (optional)
½ teaspoon freshly ground black pepper
2 small garlic cloves, minced fine
2 small scallions, chopped fine
1 medium-sized ripe, firm tomato, stem and skin removed, chopped
2 tablespoons chopped fresh dill, basil, or thyme
2 tablespoons fresh lemon juice, or dry white wine
2 small zucchini, sliced thin or diced
2 small summer squash, sliced thin or diced

1. Preheat oven to 425°F. Lay 4 pieces of aluminum foil, each 12-by-15 inches, on work surface; place one fillet crosswise in center of each piece of foil. Season fillets on both sides with salt (if desired) and pepper.

2. In medium-sized bowl, combine garlic, scallions, tomato, herb, lemon juice or wine, zucchini, and summer squash; stir to mix well. Spoon vegetable and seasoning mixture over fish, dividing it evenly.

3. Leaving space inside for steam, seal packets by folding the long ends together first, then folding sides together and turning side folds upward to reduce risk of leakage. Place packets on baking sheet.

4. Bake 15 minutes. Remove tray from oven; let packets sit 5 additional minutes. To serve, carefully open each packet, being careful to avoid release of steam. Using long spatula, transfer fish and vegetables to plates; spoon juice from packets over tops.

Easy to assemble, quick to bake—this version of en papillote answers a busy fish lover's prayers. Once you try this fail-proof technique you will probably use it frequently. For variety and a real taste treat, substitute bottled barbecue sauce for the lemon juice.

PER SERVING
CALORIES: **164**
PROTEIN: **31 grams**
FAT: **1 gram**
SODIUM: **95 milligrams**
CHOLESTEROL: **74 milligrams**

Wine-marinated Mahimahi

Also named dolphin fish, this tasty meat is an actual fish and not a marine mammal. Its firm flesh makes it an ideal choice for the grill. (You can use other firm fish if you like.) Peel ripe plantains and add to the grill for a delightful side dish.

PER SERVING

CALORIES: 170
PROTEIN: 20 grams
FAT: 9 grams
SODIUM: 53 milligrams
CHOLESTEROL: 62 milligrams

◆ 16 SERVINGS

1 cup mild olive oil
½ cup dry white wine, or freshly squeezed lemon juice
½ teaspoon ground black pepper
¼ teaspoon salt (optional)
2 bay leaves, broken
1 scallion, including green top, thinly sliced (optional)
2 cloves garlic, minced (optional)
1 tablespoon fresh chopped thyme, parsley, dill, or other herb of choice (optional), or 1 teaspoon dried herb
4 pounds 1-inch-thick mahimahi steaks, or other firm-textured fish, such as whitefish, cod, or catfish

1. In large plastic storage bag, combine olive oil, wine, pepper, salt (if desired), bay leaves, scallion, garlic, and herb; shake to mix well. Place bag in large bowl or pan; add fish to bag. Turn the bag several times to coat fish completely. To marinate, let rest 1 hour.

2. Meanwhile, prepare oiled grill for barbecuing. (Coals should be arranged around edge of grill instead of in center, to allow fish to cook by indirect heat.) Arrange fish steaks on grill, or put them in grilling basket and place on grill; reserve remaining marinade. Grill 5 minutes; brush with marinade. Using wide spatula, carefully turn steaks to other side; brush with marinade. Grill 5 additional minutes or until fish flakes when tested.

Golden Grilled Stuffed Brook Trout

♦ 4 SERVINGS

    4 small whole brook trout, dressed, deboned
 ½ teaspoon salt (optional)
    1 tablespoon lemon juice
    1 tablespoon butter or margarine
 ½ cup chopped onion
 ½ cup diced celery
 ½ cup chopped mushrooms
 1¼ cups fresh bread crumbs or packaged stuffing mix
 ½ teaspoon poultry seasoning
 ¼ teaspoon ground black pepper
 ¼ cup vegetable broth or clam juice
    2 teaspoons vegetable oil
Optional garnishes: bell peppers, celery leaves, and/or
    mushrooms

1. Prepare grill or hibachi for cooking. (Avoid chemically processed charcoal briquettes and chemical starters, which can give grilled foods an unpleasant taste.)

2. Rinse trout with cold running water; pat dry. Season inside and out with salt (if desired) and lemon juice.

3. While coals heat, heat butter in large skillet; add onion, celery, and mushrooms. Sauté until soft, about 5 minutes. Remove from heat; stir in bread crumbs, poultry seasoning, pepper, and broth. Lightly fill fish cavities with stuffing; close openings with wooden picks. Lightly brush fish and hinged wire grilling basket with a little vegetable oil; add fish and whatever garnishes you choose; close and secure basket. If grilling basket (an easy means of turning fish) is not available, wrap fish in foil pierced in several places to allow smoky flavor to penetrate.

4. When coals are covered with gray ash, grill fish about 8 minutes. Turn fish to other side and cook until fish flakes easily when tested with fork, and stuffing is cooked through.

Seldom told now are stories of long summer days at the countless brooks and streams, waters running through the South, where fathers, their daughters, and sons could spend hours in pursuit of supplement for a family meal or for the pure joy. Whatever the reason, a treasury of shiny brook trout would be an additional bonus to the legacy of rich country life and the value of family. Considered "small fry," less-than-a-pound whole trout make one serving.

PER SERVING

CALORIES: 377
PROTEIN: 35 grams
FAT: 22 grams
SODIUM: 232 milligrams
CHOLESTEROL: 105 milligrams

Escoveitched Fish

In the heat of the islands, during the prerefrigeration days, pickling was used to help foods keep. The tangy taste is so appealing that citrus-marinated fish is still a favorite throughout the Caribbean. Cut into bite-size pieces to serve as appetizers or leave whole for main dish.

PER SERVING

CALORIES: **246**
PROTEIN: **36 grams**
FAT: **7 grams**
SODIUM: **78 milligrams**
CHOLESTEROL: **62 milligrams**

◆ 6 SERVINGS

Juice of 1 lemon
Juice of 2 limes
  6 small red snappers, dressed
  4 teaspoons salt (optional)
  4 teaspoons freshly ground black pepper
½ cup vegetable oil (for pan frying)
  1 cup vinegar
  1 Scotch bonnet–type chile, cut into rings
  1 chayote, peeled and cut into julienne strips
  2 medium-sized onions, sliced
12 allspice berries
  6 whole black peppercorns

1. In large bowl, combine several cups water, lemon juice, and lime juice; in this mixture, wash snappers thoroughly. Dry fish and dust with mixture of salt (if you like) and pepper; set them aside.

2. In large skillet, heat vegetable oil and fry fish on both sides until crisp, about 3 to 5 minutes per side. Remove fish, drain, and place in shallow nonreactive bowl.

3. Prepare marinade by placing vinegar, chile, chayote, onions, allspice, and peppercorns in medium saucepan and bring to a boil over medium flame; simmer about 3 minutes. Lower heat and continue cooking until onions are tender. Remove marinade from heat, cool slightly, and pour over fish. Allow fish to rest in marinade for 1 hour to absorb all flavors.

Sparks's Scalloped Oysters

◆ 8 SERVINGS

¼ cup minced onion
¼ cup (½ stick) butter or margarine, melted
¾ teaspoon celery salt (optional)
1 tablespoon Worcestershire sauce
1 teaspoon fresh lemon juice
2 cups oyster crackers or broken saltine crackers
1 tablespoon chopped fresh parsley
1 pint container fresh standard oysters
1 cup whole milk

1. Heat oven to 350°F. In small skillet, melt butter; sauté onion several minutes until clear. Remove from heat and stir in celery salt, Worcestershire, and lemon juice.

2. Combine crackers and parsley flakes. Drain oysters, reserving ⅓ cup of liquor. Sprinkle ½ cup crumb mixture in bottom of lightly greased 1½ quart baking dish; layer on half of oysters and half of remaining cracker crumb mixture. Drizzle with half of butter mixture. Repeat layers.

3. Combine milk and reserved oyster liquor; mix well. Pour over oyster layers. Bake until lightly browned and bubbly, about 35 minutes.

Before becoming an aeronautical engineer at the Alameda Naval Air Station in California, my uncle Thomas Sparks served as a staff sergeant and chef in the United States Army. He had such a fine sense of decorum and style, it's hard to associate him in any way with a MESS hall. He reserved this rich casserole for special occasions and winter holidays.

PER SERVING

CALORIES: **237**
PROTEIN: **6 grams**
FAT: **13 grams**
SODIUM: **589 milligrams**
CHOLESTEROL: **52 milligrams**

"Big Easy" Shrimp Creole

The unique assemblage of ethnic cultures in New Orleans around the 1700s produced a cooking style that is our nation's most distinctive. This is a dish that never fails to bring raves. The recipe can be doubled, and chicken or less expensive seafood can be substituted for a portion of the shrimp. Spice this one up as much as you like.

PER SERVING
CALORIES: 248
PROTEIN: 15 grams
FAT: 6 grams
SODIUM: 477 milligrams
CHOLESTEROL: 87 milligrams

◆ 6 SERVINGS

½ cup chopped onion
½ cup chopped celery
1 garlic clove, minced
2 tablespoons vegetable oil
1-pound can (2 cups) tomatoes, drained
8-ounce can tomato sauce
½ teaspoon salt (optional)
1 teaspoon sugar
1 tablespoon Worcestershire sauce
1 teaspoon chili powder
½ teaspoon hot pepper sauce
2 small bay leaves
2 teaspoons cornstarch
12 ounces fresh shrimp, shelled and deveined
½ cup chopped green pepper
3 cups warm cooked rice

1. In skillet, cook onion, celery, and garlic in vegetable oil until tender but not brown. Add tomatoes, tomato sauce, salt (if desired), sugar, Worcestershire sauce, chili powder, hot pepper sauce, and bay leaves. Simmer uncovered 45 minutes.

2. Mix cornstarch with 1 tablespoon cold water; stir into sauce. Cook and stir until mixture thickens and bubbles. Add shrimp and green pepper. Cover; simmer 5 minutes. Discard bay leaves. Serve with rice.

Paella

◆ 6 SERVINGS

 12 mussels in shells
 ½ cup water or dry white wine (for steaming mussels)
  1 tablespoon olive oil
  1 cup cubed boneless chicken breast
  1 medium-sized yellow onion, chopped
  1 cup uncooked medium-grain or long-grain rice
  1 garlic clove, minced
1½ cups Basic Chicken Broth (page 19), All-purpose
    Vegetable Broth (page 18), or low-sodium canned
    broth
14½-ounce can tomatoes, chopped, juice saved
  4 saffron strands, or ⅛ teaspoon ground saffron
 ½ teaspoon cayenne pepper, or to taste
 ½ teaspoon salt (optional)
  1 bay leaf
 ½ pound large shrimp, peeled and deveined
  1 small green bell pepper, seeds and membranes removed,
    cut into strips
 ½ cup frozen green peas, thawed
6-ounce jar pimientos, sliced or chopped

One-pot meals of rice and a mixture of seafood and meats are prepared in kitchens around the world. This Spanish-inspired dish features the beautiful coloring and subtle flavoring of saffron and even has its own pan, bearing the same name. The shallow pan can go from the top of the range directly to guests waiting eagerly at the table.

PER SERVING

CALORIES: **267**
PROTEIN: **20 grams**
FAT: **4 grams**
SODIUM: **244 milligrams**
CHOLESTEROL: **71 milligrams**

1. Scrub mussels well; just before cooking, cut off beards. Place mussels and water or wine in large skillet with lid; bring to boil. Lower heat; cover and simmer until mussels open, about 5 minutes. Remove mussels; discard any that do not open. Drain mussel liquid through several layers of cheese-cloth; set aside.

2. Heat olive oil in 14-inch paella pan or dutch oven over medium-high heat. Add chicken; cook and stir until lightly browned. Add onion and rice; cook about 3 minutes. Add garlic; cook and stir until onion is tender and rice is lightly browned, about 3 additional minutes. Add broth (or combination of

broth and mussel liquid to equal 1½ cups), tomatoes and their juice, saffron, cayenne, salt (if desired), and bay leaf.

3. Bring to boil; stir. Reduce heat; cover and simmer 10 minutes. Add shrimp, bell peppers, peas, and pimientos; cover and simmer gently until rice is tender, about 10 minutes. Add mussels in shells; cover and let rest about 10 minutes. Discard bay leaf; serve warm.

Blue Crab Cakes with Fresh Corn Relish

◆ 4 SERVINGS

Corn Relish:

¼ cup cider vinegar

2 tablespoons sugar

½ teaspoon celery seed

¼ teaspoon mustard seed

1 cup fresh corn kernels

2 tablespoons minced red bell pepper

1 small scallion, including green top, sliced thin

3 cups cooked crabmeat (about 1 pound)

⅓ cup fresh bread crumbs or cracker crumbs

2 tablespoons mayonnaise

2 teaspoons minced parsley

1 teaspoon Worcestershire sauce

¼ teaspoon salt (optional)

½ teaspoon dry mustard

¼ teaspoon ground black pepper

1 egg, lightly beaten

2 tablespoons butter or margarine

Optional garnish: lemon wedges, fresh dill sprigs

Blue crabs are indigenous to our entire eastern shore. Smaller and somewhat tastier than the Dungeness crab from the opposite coast, the crab cakes of the Baltimore and Ohio dining cars are legendary.

PER SERVING

CALORIES: **201**

PROTEIN: **23 grams**

FAT: **10 grams**

SODIUM: **425 milligrams**

CHOLESTEROL: **168 milligrams**

1. Make corn relish ahead of time to chill before serving. In small saucepan, bring vinegar, sugar, celery seed, mustard seed, and corn to boil; reduce heat and cook about 2 minutes. Remove from heat; stir in bell pepper and scallion. Transfer to bowl; cover and chill.

2. In large bowl, pick through crabmeat to carefully remove shells. Add bread crumbs; mix gently. In small bowl combine mayonnaise, parsley, Worcestershire, salt (if desired), mustard, pepper, and egg. Stir into crabmeat and crumbs. Divide mixture into 8 portions. In 10-inch skillet over medium heat,

melt butter; spoon in 4 portions. Using pancake turner, lightly flatten portions into patties. Fry patties until golden on underside; turn and brown other side. Keep patties warm and repeat with other 4 portions. Serve crab cakes with corn relish or Tangy Tartar Sauce (page 85). Delicious served with sliced ripe tomatoes.

Seafood Lasagne

◆ 8 SERVINGS

12 lasagne noodles, uncooked
 1 teaspoon vegetable oil
 1 medium onion, chopped
 1 medium red bell pepper, chopped
 3 cloves garlic, chopped
28-ounce can crushed tomatoes with juice
 2 tablespoons tomato paste
 6 ounces small fresh shrimp, peeled, deveined, and diced
 6 ounces scallops, diced
 2 tablespoons chopped fresh basil, or 1 tablespoon dried basil
 2 cups skim milk
 2 tablespoons unbleached all-purpose flour
 2 cups 1-percent-fat cottage cheese, puréed in food processor or blender
 1 teaspoon salt (optional)
½ teaspoon ground black or cayenne pepper
Nonstick cooking spray
 1 cup shredded part-skim mozzarella cheese
½ cup grated Parmesan cheese

PER SERVING

CALORIES: **324**
PROTEIN: **28 grams**
FAT: **8 grams**
SODIUM: **788 milligrams**
CHOLESTEROL: **50 milligrams**

1. Prepare lasagne noodles according to package directions, allowing a bit less than specified time. While they are cooking, warm vegetable oil in large, nonstick saucepan over high heat. Add onion, bell pepper, and garlic; sauté 4 minutes. Stir in crushed tomatoes and tomato paste, reduce heat to low, and simmer 15 minutes, stirring often. Stir in shrimp, scallops, and basil and simmer 1 minute.

2. In small bowl, whisk together ¼ cup skim milk and flour. In large saucepan, heat remaining 1¾ cups milk until it steams. Whisk flour mixture into saucepan and continue to

cook, whisking constantly, until milk simmers and thickens. Remove from heat and whisk in cottage cheese, salt (if desired), and pepper.

3. Heat oven to 375°F. When noodles are tender but still al dente, drain well. Spray 9-by-13-inch baking dish with non-stick cooking spray. To assemble lasagne, spread ½ cup of cheese sauce on bottom of baking dish. Cover with 4 lasagne noodles. Spoon on half of tomato sauce and then ⅓ of remaining white sauce. Sprinkle with ½ cup mozzarella. Top with another 4 noodles. Spoon on rest of tomato sauce, and the remaining ½ cup mozzarella. Cover with last 4 noodles. Spread remaining white sauce on top and sprinkle with Parmesan. Bake uncovered until brown and bubbling, about 40 to 45 minutes. Let stand 10 minutes before serving.

Poached Red Snapper with Orange-Chive Sauce

◆ 10 SERVINGS

2 cups orange juice
2 cups dry white wine
1 bunch chives, coarsely chopped
1 stalk celery, sliced
½ teaspoon salt (optional)
1 teaspoon white peppercorns or ¼ teaspoon ground white pepper
3-pound whole red snapper, dressed (fillets or steaks can also be used)
Slices of citrus fruit (oranges, lemons, and/or limes)

1. In 17-inch fish poacher or covered roasting pan, combine juice, wine, 1 cup water, half the chives, all the celery, salt (if desired), and peppercorns. Place over 2 burners; bring to boil.

2. Meanwhile, rinse snapper under cold running water. Place fish on poaching rack, or place on cheesecloth for easy removal. Reduce heat in poacher nearly to a simmer. Lower fish into poaching liquid; top with remaining chives and all citrus slices. Cover and begin timing. Poach fish approximately 10 minutes per inch at thickest point. Regulate heat so broth remains continuously just below simmer (boiling liquid can break up or toughen fish). Fish is cooked when it appears white and flakes when tested.

3. Remove rack with fish; carefully transfer snapper to serving platter. If desired, make sauce from poaching liquid by straining it through layers of cheesecloth, then rapidly boiling until it reduces to desired thickness; ladle over poached fish.

This stylish dish has built-in festivity. It is perfectly suited for serving during Kwanzaa. Arrange this snapper on a platter as the menu centerpiece for the Karamu feasting on December 31 to celebrate Kuumba, the principle of creativity.

PER SERVING
CALORIES: 68
PROTEIN: 13 grams
FAT: 1 gram
SODIUM: 27 milligrams
CHOLESTEROL: 22 milligrams

Salmon Croquettes

Easy, quick, and delicious, this old standby works for breakfast, brunch, lunch, or dinner. It's not necessary to discard the bones in canned salmon; just mix them in for an added dose of calcium. Make these croquettes gourmet-style by using cooked fresh salmon or other leftover fish.

PER SERVING

CALORIES: **77**
PROTEIN: **8 grams**
FAT: **3 grams**
SODIUM: **198 milligrams**
CHOLESTEROL: **15 milligrams**

◆ 12 CROQUETTES

1 small potato, peeled and cubed
14¾-ounce can pink salmon, drained and picked over
¼ cup egg substitute
¼ cup very finely chopped onion
2 tablespoons very finely chopped red bell pepper
1 tablespoon very finely chopped fresh parsley
½ teaspoon ground red pepper
¼ cup unbleached all-purpose flour
Nonstick cooking spray

1. In medium saucepan over high heat, bring 3 cups water to boil. Add potato and boil for 10 minutes, or until tender. Drain and let cool to touch. Mash potato with fork; set aside.

2. In large bowl, combine salmon, egg substitute, onion, bell pepper, parsley, red pepper, and potato; stir well. Divide mixture into 12 portions and shape each into a 3-inch patty.

3. Place flour on plate; dredge patties with flour. Coat large skillet with nonstick cooking spray; place over medium heat. Place croquettes in skillet and cook for 1 minute on each side. Spray skillet again with cooking spray; cook patties until golden brown, about 2 minutes, turning often to prevent burning.

New and Improved Tuna Casserole

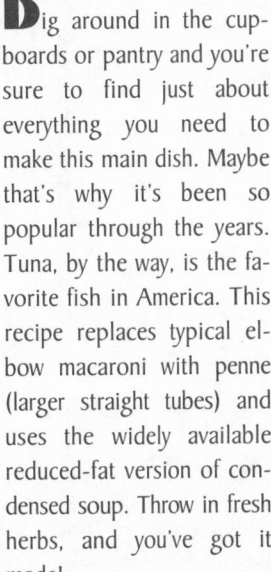

◆ 4 SERVINGS

½ teaspoon salt (optional)
 2 cups uncooked penne pasta
Nonstick cooking spray
 1 cup finely chopped onions
½ cup finely chopped green bell pepper
½ cup finely chopped red bell pepper
¼ cup chopped fresh parsley
10-ounce can 99-percent-fat-free condensed cream of
    mushroom soup
½ teaspoon granulated garlic
½ teaspoon ground red pepper
6½-ounce can tuna packed in water, drained and broken up
⅓ cup evaporated skim milk
 2 tablespoons grated Parmesan cheese

1. Heat oven to 375°F. Fill large pot ¾ full of water; cover and bring to a boil. Add salt (if desired) and penne; cook until tender, about 8 minutes. Remove from heat; drain pasta and set aside.

2. Coat medium-sized skillet with nonstick cooking spray; place over medium-high heat. Add onions, green and red bell peppers, and half of parsley; sauté for 5 minutes. Add soup, ground pepper, tuna, milk, and penne; cook and stir for 3 minutes. Remove from heat.

3. Spray inside 2-quart baking dish with nonstick cooking spray. Add pasta mixture. Sprinkle with cheese and remaining parsley. Bake about 10 minutes until bubbly and lightly browned.

Dig around in the cupboards or pantry and you're sure to find just about everything you need to make this main dish. Maybe that's why it's been so popular through the years. Tuna, by the way, is the favorite fish in America. This recipe replaces typical elbow macaroni with penne (larger straight tubes) and uses the widely available reduced-fat version of condensed soup. Throw in fresh herbs, and you've got it made!

PER SERVING

CALORIES: 336
PROTEIN: 24 grams
FAT: 4 grams
SODIUM: 489 milligrams
CHOLESTEROL: 21 milligrams

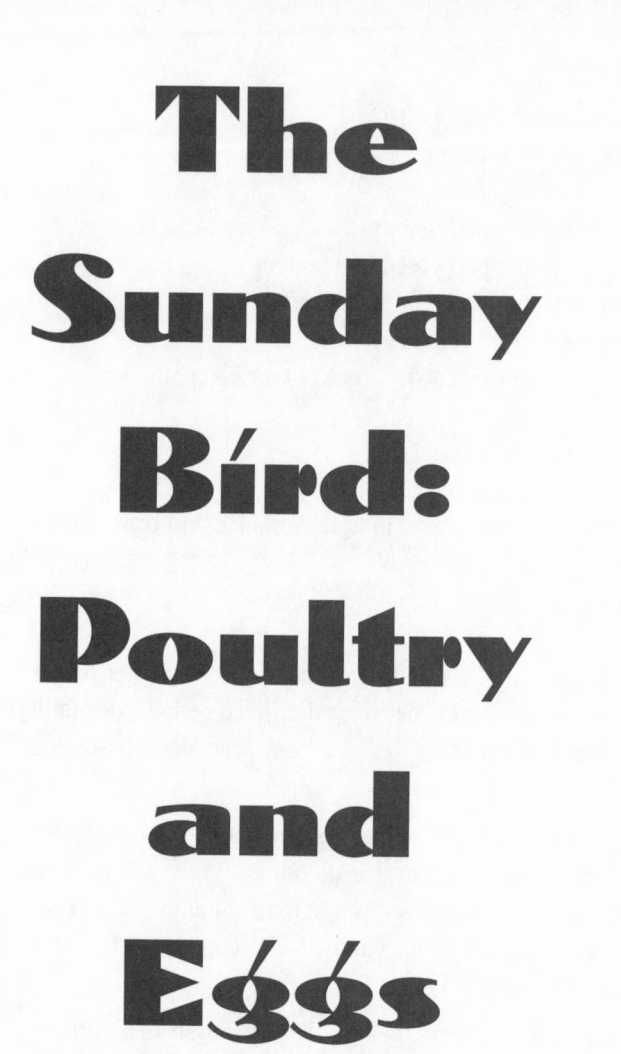

The Sunday Bird: Poultry and Eggs

Until recently, chicken was no everyday meal. It was an American symbol of prosperity—a brighter day ahead. The golden bird was reserved for Sundays, special meals, or special guests. In the South, of the many popular ways of preparing the amenable bird, frying became an art form. Whether piled high and crisp on a doily-lined silver-plated tray or packed into a shoebox for the bus ride north, fried chicken was steeped in tradition and flavor.

Black cooks of the South had such a way with frying chicken that it remains one of the legendary dishes of soulful cooking. "Secrets" to frying perfect chicken abound; time-proven methods call for a cast-iron skillet, a dip in butter-milk, and a dredge in flour—just the way our low-fat recipe is prepared in this chapter. With fewer saturated fats than most meats, the Sunday bird of hope fits a healthful eating plan. Whether you add curry powder, fresh ginger, dry wine, barbe-cue sauce, or any number of seasonings, chicken absorbs flavors beautifully and changes dramatically with different cooking techniques.

But instead of always relying on chicken, turn to turkey to add near-endless variety to meals. Its white meat is the lean-est of the lean. Ground turkey breast makes a healthful stand-in for the old standby, ground beef. And don't hesitate to break a few eggs. Just limit yolks to 3 or 4 per week. Whites contain no cholesterol and are an excellent source of protein.

SAFETY GUARDS

Don't spoil a great dinner by overlooking the risk of salmo-nella and other bacteria.

- Thaw poultry in the refrigerator rather than letting it sit at room temperature on the kitchen counter or in the sink.

Golden Roast Chicken

Skinless Fried Chicken

Crispy Baked Chicken

Island Curry Chicken and Vegetables

Momma's Old-fashioned Chicken and Dumplings

Daddy's Chicken Spaghetti

Jerk Chicken Thighs

Peachy Barbecued Cornish Hens

Chicken and Sausage Jambalaya

Chicken Nuggets with Honey-Mustard Sauce

Spicy Buffalo Chicken Rolls

Senegalese Chicken Yassa

Chicken Quesadillas

Smoked Chicken and Black Bean Salad

Party Time Curried Chicken Sandwiches

Savory Turkey Meat Loaf

Turkey Tamale Pie

Turkey Chili for a Crowd

Collard Greens Quiche

Divine Deviled Eggs

Migas

- Rinse fresh or thawed poultry inside and out with cold running water, then blot dry with paper towels.
- Use hot soapy water to wash your hands, cutting board, knife, countertop, and all items that come in contact with the raw chicken.

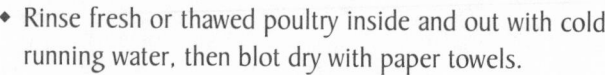

Fat Chat

◆ Get rid of the fat reservoir. Right at the tail end of the opening of the chicken cavity is a pad of fat. Pull or cut it away for leaner chicken and drippings.

◆ Remove the skin. More than half the fat in chicken is located in and under the skin. Discard skin either before cooking or before eating. If you remove it before cooking, use a moist method of cooking or baste frequently to avoid drying.

◆ Roast on a rack. Place a rack in the bottom of the roasting pan so the bird doesn't sit and cook in the fat that collects there.

◆ Marinate for soaked-in flavor. Chicken absorbs lots of flavor. Rub on a dry marinade of fresh herbs and spices, or pour on an acid-based liquid, such as lemon juice. Marinate in the refrigerator.

◆ Baste with flavorful sauces. To keep poultry moist, and to season, use fat-free liquids, such as wine, tomato juice, barbecue sauce, chicken broth, or chutney diluted with a broth.

◆ Pick light meat for leanness. White meat has 50 percent fewer grams of fat than dark.

◆ Select Cornish hens for low-fat elegance. These little birds have not had time to develop much fat. They are quick-cooking and lean, and signal a treat.

◆ When purchasing ground turkey, select breast meat with

I-percent fat. Avoid commercially packaged ground turkey that tends to have fatty dark meat and even skin ground in.

◆ Prepare egg dishes with I yolk per portion. One large egg yolk contains almost the entire daily allowance for cholesterol, approximately 213 to 220 milligrams.

THE WISHBONE

Kids today may not be familiar with the wishbone. Most chicken is now sold primarily by the part or already cut up. The butcher's blade cuts right through that horseshoe-shaped bone that girds two breast portions. It's really too bad, because when I was growing up, the wishbone belonged to a group that included shooting stars, four-leaf clovers, and rabbits' feet—it was something magical to believe in.

I usually had to compete for my wish with my sister, Marva. We followed the custom to the letter. After a Sunday dinner that was centered around a roasted chicken or capon, the bone would be retrieved intact and polished clean. We would each grasp an end, close our eyes tight, make a silent wish, then tug until the bone broke. The one left with the largest piece would have her wish come true. Since Marva was older and stronger, I never had much luck in the battle of wishes, yet there was always hope.

Golden Roast Chicken

Dining out is often described as a form of theater. The analogy proves especially true when actor-dancer-author-choreographer, painter-director-designer Geoffrey Holder cooks! As a guest chef and host at the James Beard House (a charity foundation in New York), Mr. Holder prepared a roast chicken that epitomized the succulence of foods cooked at high temperatures. His Caribbean-inspired menu began with a light first course: smoked salmon, fresh mangoes, and tomatoes. The entrée starred roasted chicken with sweet potatoes and black beans. And the finale featured ice cream with rum-soaked raisins. It was an award-winning evening. Follow these easy steps to a crispy golden bird that's sure to bring down the house.

PER SERVING

CALORIES: **280**
PROTEIN: **34 grams**
FAT: **15 grams**
SODIUM: **98 milligrams**
CHOLESTEROL: **109 milligrams**

◆ ABOUT EIGHT 3-OUNCE SERVINGS

5-pound roasting chicken
  1 tablespoon chopped fresh parsley or
    1 teaspoon dried
  1 tablespoon fresh chopped thyme or
    1 teaspoon dried
  1 teaspoon ground sage
  1 teaspoon salt (optional)
  ½ teaspoon ground black pepper
Small lemon or yellow onion, pierced several times with
  knife tip
  2 stalks celery, broken into large pieces
  1 small bunch fresh parsley
  1 teaspoon vegetable oil
  ½ cup dry red or white wine, or chicken broth

1. Remove giblets and neck from inside chicken cavity; wrap and refrigerate or freeze for future meal if you wish. Rinse bird with cold running water; drain well, then pat dry with paper towels. Mix parsley, thyme, sage, salt (if desired), and pepper; rub mixture inside body cavity and over outside. If time permits, cover and refrigerate 12 hours or overnight.

2. Preheat oven to 400°F. Fill body cavity with lemon or onion, celery, and sprigs of parsley. Lift wings up toward neck, then fold them under back of bird to lock in place and balance.

3. Tie drumsticks and tail together with string. Brush bird with vegetable oil. Place chicken, breast side up, on rack in open roasting pan or casserole dish. Pour wine or broth over chicken. Insert meat thermometer in center of thigh close to body. Roast, uncovered, about 30 minutes, basting occasionally with pan drippings.

4. Reduce oven temperature to 325°F. Roast, basting with pan drippings, about 1 additional hour. Poultry is done when thermometer reads 185°F. To test manually for doneness, protect your hand with paper towel, then gently move chicken leg up and down; it will move freely when bird is done. Transfer chicken to platter. Skim all visible fat from pan drippings; spoon remaining juice over chicken.

Skinless Fried Chicken

D anella Carter, a food and health writer, presents a delectable array of low-fat recipes in her volume of Down-Home Wholesome (Dutton). In this version of skinless frying, marinating the chicken in buttermilk makes it exceptionally moist and tender.

PER SERVING

CALORIES: **297**
PROTEIN: **30 grams**
FAT: **9 grams**
SODIUM: **362 milligrams**
CHOLESTEROL: **73 milligrams**

◆ 6 SERVINGS

6 skinless, bone-in chicken breast halves
2 cups nonfat buttermilk
½ teaspoon salt (optional)
1 teaspoon freshly ground pepper
1 tablespoon fresh lemon juice
1 teaspoon seasoned salt
2 teaspoons ground sage
2 teaspoons paprika
¼ cup finely ground cracker crumbs (saltines)
1 teaspoon baking powder
4 tablespoons vegetable oil
1 cup all-purpose flour

1. Split each halved chicken breast crosswise in half again. Place in large bowl with buttermilk; soak 1 hour. Remove chicken from buttermilk (discard buttermilk). Place chicken on deep plate; sprinkle with salt (if desired), pepper, and lemon juice; toss to mix evenly.

2. In paper bag, combine seasoned salt, sage, paprika, cracker crumbs, and baking powder; shake bag to mix. In large cast-iron or nonstick skillet, heat olive oil over medium-high heat. Dredge chicken in flour and shake off excess. When oil is very hot, lay chicken pieces in pan, fleshy side down, and immediately reduce heat to medium-low.

3. Cook 10 minutes; turn chicken over; cover and cook until golden, about 8 additional minutes. Remove and transfer to paper towels to drain.

Crispy Baked Chicken

It wasn't my intention to mimic fried chicken—this crusty chicken just turns out that way. Might as well make up a batch of biscuits and add them to the oven to bake during the last 15 minutes along with the chicken.

◆ 4 SERVINGS

2½- to 3-pound broiler-fryer chicken, cut into 8 serving
    pieces
¼ cup unbleached all-purpose flour
1 teaspoon salt (optional)
1 teaspoon freshly ground black pepper
1 teaspoon ground thyme
⅓ cup milk
2 egg whites
1½ teaspoons hot pepper sauce
1¼ cup fresh fine bread crumbs
1 teaspoon paprika

PER SERVING

CALORIES: **320**
FAT: **13 grams**
PROTEIN: **32 grams**
SODIUM: **163 milligrams**
CHOLESTEROL: **90 milligrams**

1. Cover baking sheet with waxed paper; set aside. Remove skin and any visible fat from chicken pieces.

2. In large bowl, mix flour, ½ teaspoon salt (if desired), black pepper, and thyme; set aside. In large bowl, beat together milk, whites, and pepper sauce. In large shallow dish or on waxed paper, mix bread crumbs, paprika, and remaining ½ teaspoon salt.

3. To coat chicken, dredge one piece at a time in flour mixture; dip in milk mixture, then roll in crumb mixture. Place on baking sheet. Cover with plastic wrap; refrigerate about 1 hour (to set coating).

4. Preheat oven to 350°F. Place wire rack in large shallow baking pan; arrange chicken pieces, without touching one another, on wire rack. (The rack helps prevent undersides from becoming soggy.) Bake until juice runs clear when chicken is pierced, about 45 to 55 minutes.

Island Curry Chicken and Vegetables

You just might feel the warmth of the Caribbean sun stream into your kitchen when this easy skillet meal is ready. For an additional layer of flavor, serve this spicy dish with aromatic basmati rice. Remove chicken skin before eating to cut fat and calories.

PER SERVING

CALORIES: **365**
PROTEIN: **33 grams**
FAT: **12 grams**
SODIUM: **112 milligrams**
CHOLESTEROL: **87 milligrams**

◆ 5 SERVINGS

2½- to 3-pound broiler-fryer chicken
  2 tablespoons peanut or vegetable oil (for browning chicken)
  1 medium-sized yellow onion, chopped
  1 or 2 garlic cloves, minced
1-inch piece fresh gingerroot, peeled and very thinly sliced or grated
 1½ cups fat-free chicken broth or water
  2 teaspoons curry powder, or to taste
  1 teaspoon crushed red pepper flakes
  1 cinnamon stick, about 2 inches long
 ½ teaspoon salt (optional)
Juice of ½ lemon
  2 carrots, sliced thin
  4 small red-skinned potatoes, cut into eighths
10-ounce package frozen lima beans

1. Rinse chicken inside and out with cold running water; blot dry with paper towels. Cut into 8 serving pieces. Heat peanut or vegetable oil in dutch oven or very large nonstick skillet over medium-high heat; cooking several pieces at a time, brown chicken slowly on all sides. Remove chicken; season with salt and pepper. Set aside. Pour all fat from skillet.

2. To same skillet, add onion, garlic, and ginger; cook until onion is translucent, about 8 minutes. Pour in 2 cups water; scrape up browned bits from bottom of skillet. Mix in curry powder, red pepper flakes, cinnamon, and (if desired) salt.

3. Return all chicken pieces to skillet; spoon sauce over them. Reduce heat to low; cover skillet, and simmer about 45 minutes.

4. Add lemon juice, carrots, potatoes, beans, and about ½ cup more water to skillet; cover and cook until vegetables are tender, about 20 additional minutes.

Momma's Old-fashioned Chicken and Dumplings

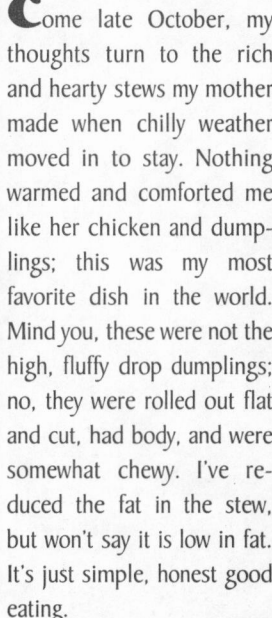

◆ 6 SERVINGS

4-pound whole chicken
1 large yellow onion, chopped coarse
2 ribs celery, chopped coarse
½ teaspoon salt (optional)
½ teaspoon freshly ground white pepper
1 bay leaf

Dumplings:

2 cups unbleached all-purpose flour
Pinch of salt (optional)
¼ cup vegetable shortening, chilled

1. Place chicken in large, heavy, broad-topped pot. Add about 2 quarts water, onion, celery, salt (if desired), pepper, and bay leaf; bring to boil over high heat. Skim off any scum. Reduce heat, cover, and simmer chicken until it is very tender, about 2 hours. Let chicken cool in stock. Remove chicken; skin and bone it. Cut or shred meat into large bite-sized pieces.

2. Degrease stock. Strain stock and return to pot.

3. To make dumplings: In large bowl, combine flour and (if desired) salt. Add vegetable shortening; cut in with pastry blender or fork until mixture resembles coarse meal. Add just enough chilled water (about 6 tablespoons) to make dough the consistency of piecrust dough. On lightly floured surface, roll out dough into large rectangle about ⅛ inch thick. Cut rectangle into strips about 4 inches long and 1½ inches wide.

Come late October, my thoughts turn to the rich and hearty stews my mother made when chilly weather moved in to stay. Nothing warmed and comforted me like her chicken and dumplings; this was my most favorite dish in the world. Mind you, these were not the high, fluffy drop dumplings; no, they were rolled out flat and cut, had body, and were somewhat chewy. I've reduced the fat in the stew, but won't say it is low in fat. It's just simple, honest good eating.

PER SERVING

CALORIES: 428
PROTEIN: 34 grams
FAT: 15 grams
SODIUM: 93 milligrams
CHOLESTEROL: 87 milligrams

4. Bring chicken broth back to a boil; drop in dough strips a few at a time. When all dough strips are in pot, add boned chicken. Reduce heat to low and simmer, uncovered, until dumplings are done, about 35 minutes. During cooking, occasionally stir gently, just enough to keep dumplings submerged and to prevent those on the bottom from sticking to pot.

Daddy's Chicken Spaghetti

◆ 5 SERVINGS

    1 pound uncooked spaghetti
    2 tablespoons olive oil
    1 medium-sized yellow onion, chopped
    1 small green bell pepper, seeds and membranes removed, chopped
    1 pound skinless, boneless chicken breast, cut into ½-inch cubes
    1 teaspoon salt (optional)
 ½ teaspoon ground white pepper
    1 teaspoon dried basil leaves, crushed
28-ounce can salt-free whole tomatoes, cut up (with liquid)
 1½ cups Basic Chicken Broth (page 19)
    3 tablespoons tomato paste

This was one of my dad's quick weekday meals. It always hit the spot.

PER SERVING

CALORIES: 482
PROTEIN: 35 grams
FAT: 3 grams
SODIUM: 105 milligrams
CHOLESTEROL: 53 milligrams

1. Cook spaghetti slightly less time than package directions indicate. Meanwhile, in 5-quart dutch oven, heat olive oil. Sauté onion and bell pepper about 5 minutes; push to one side.

2. Add chicken, salt (if desired), white pepper, and basil to dutch oven. Cook 10 minutes, stirring often. Add tomatoes, broth, and tomato paste; reduce heat to medium. Cover; cook 20 minutes, stirring often.

3. Drain cooked spaghetti; stir into sauce, mixing well. Remove from heat; let stand 10 minutes before serving.

Jerk Chicken Thighs

We all have our memories of "firsts." One of my culinary moments in time took place about four years ago when I had my first taste of authentic Jamaican jerk. I was expecting a treat but nothing that would sweep me away. The seduction took place at Peppers, an open-air restaurant in Kingston, which was the first stop of a three-city Jamaican tour. I arrived with several travel companions for drinks and dinner. My order of jerk chicken was delivered to the table in a small paper tray and with no eating utensils. Just one bite and I fell prey to its lustiness. I've had several jerk aficionados tell me that until I taste the jerk at Portland, Jamaica, the home of the Maroons who are credited with its creation, the best is yet to come. Try this quick version of a chicken dish that has become an international favorite.

PER SERVING

CALORIES: **248**
PROTEIN: **27 grams**
FAT: **14 grams**
SODIUM: **119 milligrams**
CHOLESTEROL: **98 milligrams**

◆ 4 SERVINGS

¼ cup dry red wine
2 medium-size jalapeño pepper, seeded and minced
2 tablespoons minced scallion
1 tablespoon vegetable oil
1 teaspoon ground allspice
1 garlic clove, minced
2 teaspoons fresh thyme
½ teaspoon ground cinnamon
2 tablespoons low-sodium soy sauce
½ teaspoon ground nutmeg
8 skinless chicken thighs

1. In small bowl, combine wine, jalapeño peppers, scallion, vegetable oil, allspice, garlic, thyme, cinnamon, soy sauce, and nutmeg; mix to form paste. Rub chicken evenly with seasoning paste; arrange in large shallow baking dish. Cover with plastic wrap and marinate in refrigerator at least 8 hours or overnight.

2. Heat oven to 350°F. Remove wrap. Bake chicken pieces until cooked through and fork-tender, about 45 minutes.

Peachy Barbecued Cornish Hens

◆ 4 SERVINGS

2 Cornish game hens, about I pound each
½ lemon
½ teaspoon paprika
½ teaspoon ground black pepper
½ teaspoon salt (optional)

Peachy Barbecue Sauce:

8-ounce can tomato sauce, or I cup tomato juice or
    V-8 juice
¼ cup red wine vinegar or cider vinegar
¼ cup all-fruit peach preserves
2 tablespoons Worcestershire sauce
2 tablespoons grated onion
I garlic clove, finely minced
I teaspoon chili powder
I teaspoon cayenne pepper, or to taste
I bay leaf

1. Remove giblets (save for future use if you wish) and rinse hens in cold running water; blot dry with paper towels. Using kitchen shears or sharp knife, split hens lengthwise; remove and discard any bits of fat. Rub hens with lemon; then rub with paprika, pepper, and salt (if desired). Arrange hens in shallow glass dish; cover and refrigerate up to 2 hours.

2. To prepare barbecue sauce: In medium-size saucepan, combine tomato sauce, vinegar, peach preserves, Worcester-shire, onion, garlic, chili powder, cayenne pepper, and bay leaf; mix well. Bring to boil; reduce heat to low. Simmer sauce, stirring occasionally, about 10 minutes; remove bay leaf and set aside.

3. If using charcoal grill, begin fire about 30 minutes before cooking time. Heat coals to medium heat (coals are ready

Birds of all kinds take to the grill. Just remember to baste them frequently to keep the meat from drying out. Serving Cornish hens instead of the usual burgers and chicken will go over big.

PER SERVING

CALORIES: **498**
PROTEIN: **48 grams**
FAT: **24 grams**
SODIUM: **536 milligrams**
CHOLESTEROL: **88 milligrams**

when you can hold your hand just above grid). Grill hens, skin side down, covered, about 15 minutes; baste with sauce. Turn skin side up; baste again. Continue to grill, turning and basting frequently (to prevent overcooking), until hens are tender and all traces of pink are gone from meat when cut near bone, about 20 to 30 additional minutes.

Chicken and Sausage Jambalaya

◆ 6 SERVINGS

- ½ pound Cajun-style andouille or other hot smoked sausages
- 1 pound boneless skinless chicken breasts, cut into cubes
- 1 teaspoon salt (optional)
- ½ teaspoon freshly ground black pepper
- 1 cup chopped onion
- 1 cup chopped celery
- 1 cup chopped green bell pepper
- 1 garlic clove, minced
- 1½ cups uncooked long-grain white rice
- 2 cups Basic Chicken Broth (page 19), canned low-sodium broth, or water
- 1 teaspoon dried thyme

Optional garnish: minced fresh parsley

1. Add water to a depth of about ½ inch to cast-iron dutch oven or other deep heavy pot. Slice sausage into bite-sized pieces and add to pot. Cook over medium-high heat until water boils away, about 10 minutes. Continue cooking until sausage slices are lightly browned and fat is rendered, about 8 minutes more. With a slotted spoon, remove sausage slices and reserve.

2. Pour off all but 1 tablespoon fat from pot. Season chicken with salt (if desired) and pepper. Cook in rendered sausage fat over medium heat until browned, about 5 minutes. Remove and reserve. Add onion, celery, and bell pepper to the pot; sauté until soft, about 5 minutes. Add garlic, reserved sausage and chicken, rice, chicken broth, and thyme. Bring to boil; reduce heat to low, cover, and simmer until water evaporates and rice is tender, about 15 minutes. Garnish with minced parsley.

"Jambalaya, crawfish pie, filé gumbo . . ." This lusty, rice-based dish will fill your heart with song. Orginally made with leftovers, jambalaya is as diverse and wonderful as the region that gave rise to its existence.

PER SERVING

CALORIES: **517**
PROTEIN: **32 grams**
FAT: **19 grams**
SODIUM: **447 milligrams**
CHOLESTEROL: **89 milligrams**

Chicken Nuggets with Honey-Mustard Sauce

Savory chicken morsels are a fast-food favorite that you can easily and more healthfully make at home. They are popular with kids and adults alike. Pile these nuggets on a party platter with dip and watch them disappear.

PER NUGGET WITHOUT SAUCE

CALORIES: **18**
PROTEIN: **2 grams**
FAT: **1 gram**
SODIUM: **24 milligrams**
CHOLESTEROL: **6 milligrams**

SAUCE, PER TABLESPOON

CALORIES: **8**
PROTEIN: **1 gram**
FAT: **0 grams**
SODIUM: **41 milligrams**
CHOLESTEROL: **0 milligrams**

◆ 4 OR 5 DOZEN NUGGETS

Honey-Mustard Sauce:

◆ ABOUT 1/3 CUP

2 tablespoons Dijon-style mustard
1½ tablespoons white wine vinegar
2 tablespoons honey
1/8 teaspoon freshly ground pepper
2 tablespoons snipped chives (optional)

4 chicken breast halves, boned and skinned
½ cup unseasoned dry bread crumbs
¼ cup grated Parmesan cheese
1 teaspoon salt (optional)
¼ teaspoon powdered thyme
½ cup nonfat buttermilk

1. In small bowl, combine mustard, vinegar, and honey; whisk until smooth. Season with pepper. Stir in the chives, if desired. Serve at room temperature or slightly chilled. If you make the sauce ahead, keep it refrigerated until serving time.

2. Preheat oven to 450°F. Rinse chicken with cold running water; pat dry with paper towels. Cut chicken into 1-inch "nuggets."

3. Combine bread crumbs, cheese, salt (if desired), and thyme, in shallow bowl. Dip chicken nuggets in buttermilk, then in bread crumb mixture. Place in single layer on foil-lined baking sheet. Bake 15 to 20 minutes. Serve with honey-mustard sauce.

Spicy Buffalo Chicken Rolls

◆ 4 SERVINGS

4 broiler-fryer chicken breast halves, boned and skinned
2 tablespoons butter, melted
¼ cup hot pepper sauce
5 tablespoons crumbled blue cheese
Romaine lettuce leaves
Celery leaves

1. Preheat oven to 400°F. On hard surface, using meat mallet or similar flattening utensil, gently pound chicken to ¼-inch thickness. In large glass bowl, make marinade by mixing together butter and hot-pepper sauce. Add chicken, turning to coat; cover and refrigerate 10 to 30 minutes.

2. Remove chicken from marinade; spoon 1 tablespoon of blue cheese onto center of each chicken breast. Fold in sides, then roll chicken around blue cheese. Secure with wooden picks.

3. Place chicken rolls in baking pan. Bake until chicken is fork-tender, about 30 minutes. Set oven temperature at broil or 450°F. Arrange oven or broiler rack so chicken is about 8 inches from heat. Broil about 5 minutes or until brown. Remove wooden picks and arrange lettuce and chicken on platter. Garnish with celery leaves and remaining tablespoon of blue cheese.

I've lost count of the number of cooking contests that I've judged over the years, yet my enthusiasm for the possibility of discovery that these competitions offer never wanes. Such was the case when I sampled this entry in the 1994 Delmarva Chicken Cooking Contest. I was delighted by this dish with all the flavor but none of the excess fat of the famous winged version. Created by Lisa Keys of Middlebury, Connecticut, this recipe is wonderful as a main dish or an appetizer.

PER SERVING
CALORIES: **371**
PROTEIN: **56 grams**
FAT: **15 grams**
SODIUM: **397 milligrams**
CHOLESTEROL: **169 milligrams**

Senegalese Chicken Yassa

West Africans are well known for their hospitality, and this dish of marinated chicken and onions often appears at their special occasions. Expect uniquely exciting flavors, especially delicious with rice or couscous.

◆ 4 SERVINGS

1 cup fresh lemon juice, or ½ cup red wine vinegar
2 yellow onions, sliced crosswise into ¼-inch-thick rings
3 garlic cloves, minced
1 green chile, seeds and membranes removed, minced
1 teaspoon ground white pepper
1 teaspoon salt, or to taste (optional)
3-pound chicken, cut into serving pieces
2 tablespoons peanut oil
½ cup Basic Chicken Broth (page 19)
1 bay leaf
Warm cooked rice or couscous (optional)

1. In large baking dish, combine lemon juice, onions, garlic, chile, pepper, and (if desired) salt; stir to mix well. Place chicken pieces in dish; turn to coat with mixture. Cover with plastic wrap; marinate in refrigerator at least 4 hours, turning chicken occasionally.

2. Remove chicken from marinade; pat dry with paper towels. Pour marinade through sieve set over bowl; save solids and liquid separately.

3. In large, heavy skillet, heat peanut oil; cook chicken pieces until browned on all sides, about 10 minutes. Remove from skillet; discard all but 1 teaspoon of oil. Add drained onion mixture to skillet; cook, stirring constantly, until onion is transparent, about 5 minutes.

4. Return chicken to onions in skillet, add marinade liquid, broth, and bay leaf. Bring to boil; lower heat to simmer. Cook, partially covered, until chicken is cooked through and of desired tenderness, 40 minutes or longer. Discard bay leaf.

Chicken Quesadillas

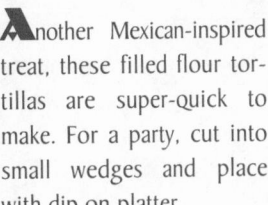

♦ 4 SERVINGS

Green Chile Dip:

⅓ cup nonfat sour cream
1 green onion, including top, sliced
¼ cup diced green chiles
2 tablespoons chopped cilantro
¼ teaspoon dried leaf oregano
⅛ teaspoon garlic salt

2 teaspoons butter or margarine
Four 8-inch flour tortillas
1 cup finely chopped chicken
¼ cup diced green chiles
½ cup shredded Monterey Jack cheese
Optional garnish: cilantro sprigs

Another Mexican-inspired treat, these filled flour tortillas are super-quick to make. For a party, cut into small wedges and place with dip on platter.

PER SERVING

CALORIES: **268**
PROTEIN: **18 grams**
FAT: **11 grams**
SODIUM: **480 milligrams**
CHOLESTEROL: **49 milligrams**

1. To prepare green chile dip: Process all ingredients in food processor until smooth. Cover and refrigerate 1 hour.

2. For each quesadilla, melt ½ teaspoon butter in wide skillet with nonstick finish over medium heat. Place 1 tortilla in pan. When tortilla is slightly warm, place ¼ cup of the chicken, 1 tablespoon of the green chiles, and 2 tablespoons of the cheese on half of tortilla.

3. Fold tortilla over filling to make a half circle. Cook, turning as needed, until cheese is melted and tortilla is lightly browned on both sides, 2 to 3 minutes. Remove from pan and keep warm. Repeat with remaining tortillas, adding 1 teaspoon butter to pan for each quesadilla. Cut each quesadilla into 3 pie-shaped wedges. Serve with chile dip.

Smoked Chicken and Black Bean Salad

This is a great party salad—quick, economical, and a crowd pleaser. Short on time? Use canned beans.

◆ 8 SERVINGS

1½- pound piece smoked chicken or turkey breast or 2 whole chicken breasts, poached or grilled, skin removed
1 cup fresh or frozen corn kernels
2 small ripe tomatoes, diced
2 small scallions, including green tops, sliced thin
3 garlic cloves, minced
1¼ serrano chiles, seeded and minced
1½ cups cooked black beans
4 tablespoons fresh lime juice
3 tablespoons olive oil
¼ teaspoon salt (optional)
¼ cup chopped cilantro
Freshly ground black pepper, to taste
Optional garnish: lettuce leaves, baked tortilla chips

1. Cut cooked chicken breasts into cubes or thin strips. In large bowl, combine chicken, corn, tomatoes, scallions, red onions, garlic, chiles, and black beans.

2. In small bowl, whisk together lime juice, vinegar, oil, and (if desired) salt. Drizzle dressing over salad mixture; toss to coat. Add cilantro and toss. Season with pepper to taste. Serve on a lettuce-lined platter with baked tortilla chips.

Party Time Curried Chicken Sandwiches

◆ 3 DOZEN

    2 cups finely chopped cooked chicken
    1 cup nonfat mayonnaise dressing
    1 teaspoon curry powder
    1 rib celery, chopped fine
    ½ green apple, chopped fine
    36 party rye or pumpernickel bread slices, crusts trimmed,
        if desired
Optional garnishes: flat parsley leaves, thin red bell
        pepper strips

Mix together chicken, mayonnaise, curry, celery, and apple until well blended. Cover each bread slice with heaping table-spoonful of chicken mixture. Garnish with parsley and thin red pepper strips, if desired.

From small simple gatherings to wedding receptions, these open-face sandwiches are party pleasers.

PER SANDWICH

CALORIES: **24**
PROTEIN: **2 grams**
FAT: **1 gram**
SODIUM: **109 milligrams**
CHOLESTEROL: **5 milligrams**

Savory Turkey Meat Loaf

Switch and save: Ground turkey breast has up to 50 percent less saturated fat than other ground meats.

◆ 10 SERVINGS

1 tablespoon vegetable oil
1 medium-sized yellow onion, chopped
2 scallions, including green tops, chopped
2 cloves garlic, minced
2 medium-size carrots, chopped fine
1 stalk celery, chopped fine
1 small green bell pepper, seeded and chopped fine
2 egg whites
½ teaspoon salt (optional)
½ teaspoon ground black pepper
¼ teaspoon cayenne pepper
½ cup catsup
½ cup skim milk
2 pounds ground turkey
¾ cup fine dry bread crumbs

1. In medium-sized nonstick skillet, heat vegetable oil; add onion, scallions, garlic, carrots, celery, and bell pepper. Sauté about 5 minutes; let vegetable mixture cool.

2. Preheat oven to 350°F. In large bowl, combine egg whites, salt (if desired), black pepper, cayenne, ¼ cup catsup, and milk; using whisk or fork, beat until blended. Add turkey, crumbs, and cooled vegetables to egg mixture; using wooden spoon or hands, mix ingredients together just until uniform.

3. Lightly pack mixture into 9-by-5-by-3-inch loaf pan, slightly rounding top. Pour remaining ¼ cup catsup over top. Bake 60 minutes; let stand 15 minutes before slicing.

Turkey Tamale Pie

◆ 6 SERVINGS

2 teaspoons vegetable oil
I small yellow onion, chopped
½ cup diced green bell pepper
2 garlic cloves, minced
14½-ounce can tomatoes, chopped (save juice)
2 cups diced or shredded cooked turkey breast
I cup cooked whole-kernel corn, drained
½ cup sliced pitted ripe olives
I tablespoon ground mild red chile
½ teaspoon ground cumin
½ teaspoon dried leaf oregano
½ teaspoon salt (optional)
Nonstick cooking spray

Cornmeal Topping:

½ cup yellow cornmeal
I½ cups skim milk
I tablespoon corn oil
¼ teaspoon salt (optional)
I large egg, lightly beaten
½ cup shredded low-fat Cheddar cheese (optional)

Tamales can be traced back to the Aztecs, who made corn-husk-wrapped bundles of seasoned meat and vegetables as offerings to the gods. This new-day tamale pie is a tantalizing and eye-appealing dish to put before party guests.

PER SERVING
CALORIES: **249**
PROTEIN: **20 grams**
FAT: **9 grams**
SODIUM: **260 milligrams**
CHOLESTEROL: **69 milligrams**

1. Preheat oven to 375°F. Heat vegetable oil in large skillet over medium heat. Add onion; sauté about 3 minutes. Add bell pepper and garlic; cook until onion is soft but not brown, about 3 additional minutes. Add tomatoes and juice to pan; stir in turkey, corn, olives, ground chile, cumin, oregano, and (if desired) salt. Simmer 10 minutes. Turn into shallow 2-quart casserole dish coated with nonstick cooking spray.

2. To make topping: In mixing bowl, combine cornmeal and ½ cup of skim milk. In medium-sized saucepan, heat remaining I cup milk over medium heat. Stir in cornmeal mixture;

cook, stirring, until cornmeal is thick, about 3 to 4 minutes. Stir in corn oil and (if desired) salt. Stir a little of hot cornmeal into beaten egg. Add egg mixture to pan; mix well. Spoon cornmeal mixture over turkey; sprinkle with cheese.

3. Bake pie until knife inserted in center of topping comes out clean, about 45 minutes.

Turkey Chili for a Crowd

◆ 15 SERVINGS

¼ cup olive oil

3 pounds ground turkey breast

4 medium-sized yellow onions, chopped

8 cloves garlic, minced

1 large green bell pepper, seeded and chopped

½ teaspoon cayenne pepper

¼ cup chili powder

1 teaspoon dried oregano

1 teaspoon coriander

1 teaspoon ground cumin

Three 16-ounce cans kidney beans, drained

1 pound, 12-ounce can chopped tomatoes, with liquid

2 cups canned tomato juice

2 cups chicken broth

1 teaspoon salt, or to taste (optional)

2 teaspoons freshly ground black pepper

½ teaspoon crushed hot red chile peppers

½ cup roughly chopped cilantro

Optional toppings: chopped tomatoes, chopped scallions, minced red onions, shredded smoked cheese or Cheddar cheese, low-fat sour cream, chopped ripe (black) olives, sliced pickled jalapeños, minced fresh cilantro

When the Black Cowboy Association and their posse rode into Gotham several years ago for their annual rodeo, the menu I created for an informal gathering in their honor included chili with an array of toppings to individualize each serving. Guests just love choices—having it their way adds to the fun. Preparing party chili the day before improves the flavor and makes the day itself less hectic.

PER SERVING

CALORIES: **246**
PROTEIN: **32 grams**
FAT: **9 grams**
SODIUM: **542 milligrams**
CHOLESTEROL: **80 milligrams**

1. In large, heavy, nonreactive pot or dutch oven, heat olive oil over medium heat and sauté turkey until cooked through and browned, mashing with fork to break up large chunks. Transfer to medium bowl, leaving about 2 tablespoons liquid in pot.

2. In same pot, sauté onions, garlic, and green pepper until soft, about 5 minutes. Add cayenne, chili powder, oregano, coriander, and cumin and cook 2 minutes, stirring occasionally.

3. Stir in beans, chopped tomatoes with their liquid, tomato juice, chicken broth, and turkey. Simmer, uncovered, over

low heat, stirring occasionally, about 45 minutes. Season chili with salt (if desired) and peppers; add ¼ cup of cilantro. Spoon into heated bowls and garnish with remaining ¼ cup cilantro. Place your choices of toppings in small bowls so guests can serve themselves.

Collard Greens Quíche

◆ 8 SERVINGS

Basic Piecrust (page 189) for 9- or 10-inch pie

  4 large eggs
  1 cup 1-percent-fat milk
  ½ teaspoon salt (optional)
  ½ teaspoon ground black pepper or cayenne pepper
  ½ teaspoon dried oregano
  ¼ cup grated onion
  ½ cup chopped red bell pepper
  1½ cups chopped cooked fresh or frozen collard greens, drained and squeezed dry
  ½ cup shredded fat-reduced Cheddar cheese or Swiss cheese

The French classic enjoys an African American translation. Collards up the flavor and the vitamin C. Fat and calories are reduced by replacing the cream with milk and using fewer eggs. Bon appétit, y'all.

PER SERVING
CALORIES: **192**
PROTEIN: **9 grams**
FAT: **10 grams**
SODIUM: **153 milligrams**
CHOLESTEROL: **113 milligrams**

1. Heat oven to 375°F for metal pan or 350°F for glass pan. Roll out dough; transfer to 9- or 10-inch quiche dish or pie pan. Ease dough into bottom and up sides; tuck edges under and crimp. Using fork, prick bottom and sides. Partially bake until crust is just beginning to color, about 12 minutes. Let cool slightly.

2. In large bowl, lightly beat eggs and milk. Add salt (if desired), black or cayenne pepper, oregano, onion, green pepper, and collard greens; set aside.

3. Sprinkle half of cheese on piecrust. Carefully pour egg mixture on top of cheese. Sprinkle remaining cheese on top. Bake until knife inserted halfway between center and outside edge comes out clean, about 45 to 60 minutes. Let rest 10 minutes before cutting into wedges.

Divine Deviled Eggs

Before the unwarranted egg scare, spicy stuffed eggs were one of our party and picnic favorites. This tasty, health-conscious version will, I hope, put them back on the table.

PER HALF EGG

CALORIES: **51**
PROTEIN: **3 grams**
FAT: **4 grams**
SODIUM: **48 milligrams**
CHOLESTEROL: **108 milligrams**

◆ 12 HALVES

 6 large hard-cooked eggs, peeled
 3 to 4 tablespoons low- or no-fat mayonnaise
 1 teaspoon Dijon mustard, or to taste
¼ cup finely chopped celery
¼ cup finely chopped turkey ham (optional)
¼ teaspoon salt (optional)
¼ teaspoon cayenne pepper or white pepper
Paprika
Optional garnishes: red caviar, chopped or slivered ripe olives, chopped pimiento, capers, chopped scallions, watercress leaves

1. Halve eggs lengthwise. Cut thin slice from bottom of each half so eggs will sit flat. Chop trimmings and reserve.

2. Remove yolks gently; place in small bowl with trimmings. Using fork, mash yolks and trimmings. Add mayonnaise, mustard, celery, turkey ham (if you wish), salt (if desired), and pepper; stir until well mixed but not mushy.

3. Using spoon or piping bag, fill hollow of each egg half with yolk mixture. Sprinkle with paprika. Add additional garnishes of choice.

Mígas

◆ 4 SERVINGS

3 eggs
3 egg whites
½ cup grated low-fat Monterey Jack cheese
¼ teaspoon salt (optional)
¼ teaspoon ground black pepper
1 tablespoon vegetable oil
1 small white onion, minced
1 large tomato, diced
1 small jalapeño, seeds and membranes removed, minced
4 corn tortillas, cut in strips
Optional garnishes: black beans, salsa

1. In medium bowl, beat eggs, egg whites, cheese, salt (if desired), and pepper just until mixed; set aside.

2. In large nonstick skillet, heat vegetable oil; sauté onion until clear. Stir in tomato and jalapeño; cook about 5 minutes. Add tortilla strips; cook about 3 minutes. Add beaten egg mixture to ingredients in skillet. Over low heat, cook and stir until creamy yet firm (do not dry out). Serve with warm tortillas, black beans, and salsa.

Corn tortillas (perhaps the simplest form of corn bread) are sliced and scrambled with eggs and onion for this company-worthy main dish. The secret to thick and creamy scrambled eggs is to cook them slowly and keep a watchful eye. Remove the skillet from the burner a few seconds ahead of time, because eggs will continue to cook away from the heat. Follow tradition by serving this Tex-Mex favorite with black beans and salsa. Fresh orange juice with a jigger of tequila, if you like, goes along well.

PER SERVING
CALORIES: **248**
PROTEIN: **14 grams**
FAT: **14 grams**
SODIUM: **243 milligrams**
CHOLESTEROL: **170 milligrams**

Meaty Ideas

On big summer holidays when I was growing up in Detroit, the passion, aroma, and smoke of barbecuing would engulf the entire neighborhood. Spareribs ruled the day. And when it came time for dinner, I thought the Fourth of July was even better than long-awaited Christmas. Eating at our backyard picnic table sure beat the dining room. Outdoors, no one cared if you laughed with your mouth full of half-chewed corn, or licked your fingers. Daddy's barbecued ribs were without compare—the taste was transcendental. Over carefully tended coals, he cooked the slabs to perfection, dabbing them with a magic sauce he made himself.

These days, "cue" is only nostalgia for me. It's been almost two decades since I ate my last sparerib or dish of pork. I eat beef or a small piece of lamb occasionally, a reflection of how my way of eating has evolved.

As you find your own path to a healthy course of eating, it may come as a relief to know that you don't have to give up red meat to be your best. Somewhere along the spectrum between those who feel a meal without meat is not really a meal and the vegans (strict vegetarians) who flinch at the mention of meat, you can find a point of moderation that is true to your personal reality. In fact, meat provides a number of essential nutrients—iron, zinc, protein, and five of the B-complex vitamins. For women who need to pump up their iron intake to meet the recommended 15 milligrams per day (which exceeds the amount needed by men), meat is a good source. Although you can get iron from many food sources, the body absorbs the heme iron (the source of hemoglobin) supplied by red meat more readily than the iron from plant sources. To make the most of meat, however, you must minimize its nutritional downside—the high fat content.

Until recently, the more marbling (small flecks of fat throughout the lean) beef had, the better its grade and the

Wine-braised Pot Roast

◆

Texas Barbecued Beef Brisket

◆

Barbecued Short Ribs

◆

Cubed Steaks with
Creole Sauce

◆

Savory Pepper Steak

◆

Gingery Beef and
Broccoli Stir-Fry

◆

Overstuffed Bell Peppers

◆

Weekday Beef and
Macaroni Skillet

◆

Saucy Barbecued Beef
Sandwiches

◆

Lamb Curry with Sweet
Mango Chutney

◆

Sausage with Kale
and Potatoes

higher its price. "Prime" was tops, followed by "choice," then "select." Now "select" (because it's lower in fat) may be considered best, which only proves that those family-pleasing, old-fashioned, slow-cooked pot roasts with root vegetables and natural gravy were even better than we knew! In addition to more flavor, these lean, less tender cuts yield more meat per pound for less money.

For those of you with a taste for pork, even Ms. Piggy has trimmed down. The new breeds of pork contain as few as 4.1 grams fat per 3-ounce serving, making them lower in fat than some cuts of beef and even skinless chicken thighs.

So you see, there's no need to steer clear of meat. Enjoy it as a bold seasoning ingredient rather than as the focus of the meal. Stir-fries, stews, and casseroles that combine meat with greater amounts of fresh vegetables, robust grains, or the many shapes of pasta make hearty home-style meals with lots of flavor and appeal, and little fat.

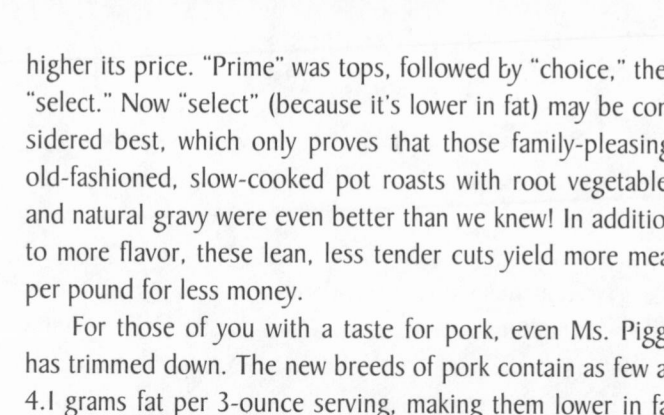

Fat Chat
Meat can fit into a healthy diet when you streamline it.

◆ Choose the leanest cuts. The smart beef choices are round or rump cuts—top round (London broil), eye of the round, round tip, and flank steaks, or sirloin tip, top sirloin, or tenderloin. Pork fanciers also have a range of lower-fat choices: tenderloin, loin roasts and chops, and 95-percent lean ham. Be sure to trim off any visible fat.

◆ Know your numbers when selecting ground beef. Meat labeled "hamburger" can contain up to 33 percent pure fat. At the opposite end of the scale is 96-percent-lean ground beef, which is 4 percent fat by weight, translating to 1 gram of fat per ounce.

◆ Use heavyweight, nonstick skillets and cookware as much as possible. An obvious saving, because with these utensils there's no need to add oil to prevent sticking.

◆ Cook to defat. Instead of adding fat by deep- or pan-frying, broil or grill, methods which actually melt and drain off the fat within the meat. To be effective, the meat must broil on a rack over a pan.

◆ Brown without adding fat. Use nonstick cooking spray to coat the bottom of a nonstick skillet or pot, then heat the skillet and brown the meat as usual. If the meat sticks, simply add a teaspoon or two of water, broth, or juice and loosen with a spatula.

◆ Marinate lean (less tender) cuts. Reduce oil called for in marinades to no more than I tablespoon per ½ cup, or eliminate the oil altogether. Citrus juices, vinegar, and other acidic liquids add flavor and help tenderize meats before cooking.

◆ Stretch ground meat in meat loaf and burgers. Stir in shredded raw vegetables, such as carrots and zucchini, or add cooked rice, mashed potatoes, or mashed cooked beans to reduce the amount of fat per serving.

◆ Create natural gravy. After baking or roasting meat, degrease the drippings by letting it rest for a short time, then spoon off the surface fat.

◆ Switch from ultrafatty bacon and ham hocks to turkey bacon and turkey ham to add smoky flavor to dried beans and vegetables. Canadian bacon is also a leaner choice.

◆ Do not salt meat before cooking. Salt can delay browning and draw out natural flavor and juices.

◆ Limit portions to 3-ounce servings. That's about 4 ounces of meat before cooking. As a gauge, a portion should be roughly the size of a deck of playing cards. If you're thinking that it's not much, you're on the right track.

Wine-braised Pot Roast

This pot roast makes a one-time, savory main dish for eight people. If there are fewer of you, plan on spin-off sandwiches, salads, or other great meals. The rich brown gravy goes well with rice, egg noodles, and boiled or mashed potatoes. Add spinach, kale, or string beans to round out the menu beautifully.

PER SERVING

CALORIES: **211**
PROTEIN: **28 grams**
FAT: **7 grams**
SODIUM: **90 milligrams**
CHOLESTEROL: **63 milligrams**

◆ 8 SERVINGS

3-pound boneless beef shoulder chuck roast
 2 garlic cloves, minced
 2 tablespoons unbleached all-purpose flour
 2 tablespoons vegetable oil
 1 cup red burgundy or other dry red wine
13-ounce can reduced-sodium beef broth
 1 teaspoon dried leaf oregano
 1 bay leaf
 ½ pound fresh mushrooms, cleaned and sliced
 ½ teaspoon salt (optional)
 ½ teaspoon ground black pepper

1. Trim and discard visible fat from roast; wipe meat with damp paper towels. Rub roast with garlic. On waxed paper, coat evenly with flour.

2. In dutch oven, heat vegetable oil over medium-high heat. Add roast and cook, turning often, until browned on all sides. Pour off all fat.

3. Add wine, broth, oregano, and bay leaf. Bring liquid to boil; reduce heat to low simmer. Cover tightly and cook about 2 hours, turning occasionally. Add mushrooms, salt (if desired), and pepper. Cook until roast is fork-tender, about 30 additional minutes.

4. Transfer meat to cutting board. Discard bay leaf. Skim any fat from surface of gravy in pot. To thicken gravy, cook over medium-high heat until reduced, as desired. To thin gravy, add more broth, wine, or water; simmer several minutes to blend and heat through.

Texas Barbecued Beef Brisket

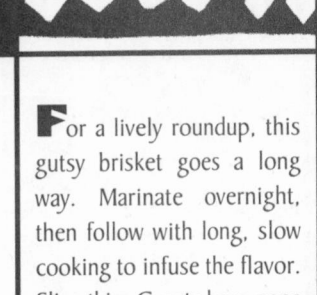

◆ 12 SERVINGS

4-pound boneless fresh beef brisket (not corned)
 2 large garlic cloves, halved lengthwise
 2 packed tablespoons brown sugar
 1 tablespoon cracked black pepper
 1 teaspoon ground cumin
 1 teaspoon salt (optional)
 1 teaspoon dried leaf oregano
 ½ teaspoon cayenne pepper
 ¼ cup reduced-sodium beef broth
Juice of 1 lime
 1 cup barbecue sauce, homemade or bottled

1. Trim and discard visible fat from brisket; wipe meat with damp paper towels. Rub brisket with cut sides of garlic; place in 13-by-9-inch baking dish.

2. In bowl, combine brown sugar, black pepper, cumin, salt (if desired), oregano, and cayenne; mix well. Stir in beef broth and lime juice; blend. Pour seasoning mix over meat; turn meat to coat. Cover tightly with foil; refrigerate overnight or up to 24 hours.

3. Preheat oven to 325°F. Bake, covered, about 3½ hours or until very tender when pierced with fork. Remove from oven; remove foil. Let stand 10 minutes. Transfer meat to cutting board; cover to keep warm.

4. Pour pan juices into glass measuring cup or into fat-separating cup. Skim or pour off fat and discard. Pour drippings into small saucepan; stir in barbecue sauce. Simmer about 5 minutes. Slice meat across grain; arrange on platter. Drizzle sauce over meat.

For a lively roundup, this gutsy brisket goes a long way. Marinate overnight, then follow with long, slow cooking to infuse the flavor. Slice thin. Guests have gone hog wild when served this robust dish with black or baked beans, coleslaw, corn bread, and pitchers of beer or iced tea. Brisket also makes a great filling for sandwiches, tacos, and enchiladas.

PER SERVING

CALORIES: **317**
PROTEIN: **33 grams**
FAT: **15 grams**
SODIUM: **264 milligrams**
CHOLESTEROL: **104 milligrams**

Barbecued Short Ribs

After all, what kind of a summer would it be without barbecued ribs? Fire up the grill! Even for those who don't eat pork, there's tradition and ritual to uphold. These precooked beef short ribs provide considerably more meat and much less fat than traditional spareribs. Picnic Potato Salad (page 52) and lemonade are musts. The other dishes are up to you.

PER SERVING

CALORIES: **329**
PROTEIN: **33 grams**
FAT: **17 grams**
SODIUM: **252 milligrams**
CHOLESTEROL: **82 milligrams**

◆ 8 SERVINGS

5 to 6 pounds beef chuck short ribs

Barbecue Sauce:

Nonstick cooking spray
½ cup finely chopped yellow onion
1 garlic clove, minced
2 tablespoons brown sugar
2 tablespoons cider vinegar or aged or flavored vinegar
½ teaspoon ground black pepper
½ cup catsup
1 teaspoon Worcestershire sauce
½ cup reduced-sodium beef broth

1. Trim and discard visible fat from meat; wipe with damp paper towels. In 8-quart dutch oven, cover beef short ribs with water. Over high heat, bring to boil. Reduce heat to low; cover and simmer until ribs are fork-tender, about 2 hours.

2. Meanwhile, about 1 hour before serving time, prepare outdoor grill for barbecuing. Heat coals to moderate temperature. Grilling over moderate coals (300°F to 350°F) is best for even cooking and to prevent charring. To check temperature, use a flat-surface oven thermometer or the tried-and-true hand test: Place your hand at cooking height, just above grill rack. If you can hold it there for 3 to 4 seconds, the heat is moderate.

3. To make barbecue sauce, coat small skillet with nonstick cooking spray; sauté onion and garlic. Stir in brown sugar, vinegar, and pepper until sugar dissolves. Stir in catsup, Worcestershire sauce, and broth; simmer, stirring occasionally, about 15 minutes.

4. On grill rack coated with nonstick cooking spray, arrange cooked ribs. Brush generously with sauce; turn and baste frequently until ribs are nicely browned and heated through.

Cubed Steaks with Creole Sauce

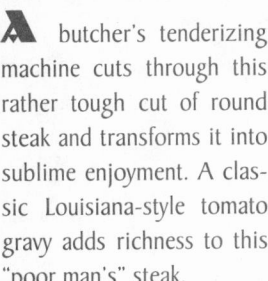

◆ 5 SERVINGS

1¼ pounds beef cubed steaks
 2 tablespoons vegetable oil
 1 tablespoon all-purpose flour
 1 small yellow onion, chopped
 1 small green bell pepper, seeds and membranes removed,
   chopped
 1 rib celery, sliced thin
 3 medium-sized tomatoes, chopped
 1 tablespoon fresh thyme leaves or 1 teaspoon dried thyme
 1 teaspoon sugar
 ½ teaspoon salt (optional)
 ½ teaspoon ground black pepper
 1 bay leaf
 1 tablespoon chopped fresh parsley

A butcher's tenderizing machine cuts through this rather tough cut of round steak and transforms it into sublime enjoyment. A classic Louisiana-style tomato gravy adds richness to this "poor man's" steak.

PER SERVING

CALORIES: **226**
PROTEIN: **28 grams**
FAT: **8 grams**
SODIUM: **68 milligrams**
CHOLESTEROL: **72 milligrams**

1. Trim and discard visible fat from steaks; wipe meat with damp paper towels. In large nonstick skillet, heat vegetable oil; add steaks without overlapping (cook in batches if necessary). Cook until browned, about 3 minutes on each side. Remove browned steaks from skillet; set aside.

2. Remove and discard all but 1 tablespoon oil from skillet. Stir in flour; cook and stir until flour begins to brown. Add onion, bell pepper, and celery; stir and cook until onion is transparent, scraping up browned bits from skillet, about 5 minutes. Stir in tomatoes, thyme, sugar, salt (if desired), pepper, bay leaf, and ½ cup hot water; mix well. Over low heat, simmer, stirring occasionally, about 10 minutes.

3. Return steaks to skillet; spoon sauce over meat and sprinkle with parsley. Over low heat, cover and cook just until steaks are heated through. Discard bay leaf.

Savory Pepper Steak

It's not surprising that Chinese restaurants seem at home in many of our neighborhoods. Their inspired one-pot dishes with well-seasoned sauces (gravy), served over rice, connect with our own culinary roots. This simple recipe for beef smothered with bell peppers and onions will rival your favorite takeout.

◆ 6 SERVINGS

1¼ pounds lean boneless beef top round steak
1 tablespoon peanut oil
2 small bell peppers (use 1 red, 1 green for a prettier presentation), seeds and membranes removed, cut into ½-inch-wide strips
1 medium-sized yellow onion, sliced lengthwise
2 garlic cloves, minced
1 teaspoon ground ginger
½ teaspoon dried red pepper flakes
¼ teaspoon freshly ground black pepper
1½ cups reduced-sodium beef broth
1 tablespoon cornstarch
½ teaspoon sugar
2 tablespoons reduced-sodium soy sauce
1 tablespoon rice vinegar or balsamic vinegar
3 cups warm cooked rice (optional)
Optional garnish: diagonally sliced scallions (including green tops)

1. Trim and discard excess fat from steak. For easier slicing, place steak in freezer for 30 minutes; remove and slice across grain into very thin strips 2 to 3 inches long.

2. In large nonstick skillet or wok, heat ½ tablespoon peanut oil; rotate pan to coat evenly. Add bell peppers and onion; sauté until edges of onion begin to brown. Remove vegetables and keep warm. Add remaining ½ tablespoon peanut oil to skillet; heat until hot. Add beef and garlic; stir vigorously and cook until meat is browned. Season with ginger, red pepper flakes, and black pepper. Stir in 1 cup broth. Cover and simmer over low heat about 20 minutes.

3. Return peppers and onion to skillet; mix with beef. In small bowl, blend remaining ½ cup broth, cornstarch, sugar, soy sauce, and vinegar. Add broth mixture to skillet; stir until well mixed and sauce thickens. Cook about 1 additional minute. Delicious served over rice.

Gingery Beef and Broccoli Stir-Fry

Stir-fry meals are ready in a flash. Have all ingredients sliced, diced, and measured before you begin cooking. Cook meat in batches so it doesn't steam. If you're not familiar with fresh gingerroot, you're in for a treat— a burst of spicy aroma and sweet peppery flavor. Look for a "hand" with smooth, crisp skin. Use a small paring knife or vegetable peeler to remove the root's paperlike peel; then grate or slice. Serve your stir-fry dish over baked potatoes, noodles, or rice.

PER SERVING

CALORIES: **260**
PROTEIN: **29 grams**
FAT: **12 grams**
SODIUM: **474 milligrams**
CHOLESTEROL: **76 milligrams**

◆ 4 SERVINGS

12 ounces boneless beef top sirloin steak or top round (about 1 inch thick)
1 tablespoon reduced-sodium soy sauce
1 teaspoon roasted sesame oil
2 tablespoons grated fresh ginger
1 large garlic clove, minced
½ teaspoon red pepper flakes

Sauce:

¼ cup water or beef broth
2 tablespoons dry sherry
2 tablespoons reduced-sodium soy sauce
1 tablespoon cornstarch
1 tablespoon vegetable oil
1 head broccoli, stems removed (save for soup stock), head cut into florets
1 small red bell pepper, seeds and membranes removed, cut into strips
Optional garnishes: thinly sliced scallion (including green top), toasted sesame seeds

1. Trim and discard fat from steak; wipe meat with damp paper towels. Cut steak lengthwise in half; cut crosswise in ⅛-inch-thick (very thin) strips. In food storage bag, combine soy sauce, sesame oil, ginger, garlic, and red pepper flakes. Add beef strips; seal bag, squeezing out air. Rotate bag to coat meat; refrigerate 1 hour, turning bag occasionally.

2. Meanwhile, prepare sauce: In small bowl, combine water or broth, sherry, soy, and cornstarch; set aside.

3. Add ½ tablespoon vegetable oil to large nonstick skillet or wok; rotate pan to coat evenly. Heat until hot. Add marinated beef (cook half at a time); stir vigorously and cook until meat is no longer pink, about 3 minutes. Remove with slotted spoon and keep warm.

4. Add remaining ½ tablespoon vegetable oil to skillet. Add broccoli florets and bell pepper; stir-fry about 3 to 4 minutes. Add 1 tablespoon water; cover and steam until crisp-tender. Stir in cooked beef.

5. Give sauce mixture a good stir and add; cook and stir until sauce is thickened and bubbly, about 2 minutes. Serve right away; sprinkle with scallion and sesame seeds, if desired.

Overstuffed Bell Peppers

Beef plays only a supporting role in this hearty main dish; the real stars are the fresh vegetables and fluffy rice. During the summer, brilliantly colored red, orange, and yellow peppers cost little more than the green variety, so snap up a mix of colors for an exciting presentation. You'll want to add this flavorful classic to your culinary repertoire.

◆ 6 SERVINGS

6 large green (or other) bell peppers
Nonstick cooking spray
1 pound 96-percent-lean ground beef
1 small yellow onion, chopped fine
2 ribs celery, sliced thin
1 tablespoon chili powder
½ teaspoon ground black pepper
½ teaspoon salt (optional)
3 cups cooked Basic Brown Rice (page 65)
1 large carrot, shredded
½ cup shredded reduced-fat Cheddar cheese
2 cups tomato juice or tomato sauce

1. Preheat oven to 350°F. Cut sliver from bottom of each pepper so they will stand upright. Cut tops from peppers; remove seeds and membranes. Set aside.

2. Coat large skillet with nonstick cooking spray. Over medium heat, cook beef, separating into smaller pieces, until no longer pink. Add onion, celery, chili powder, black pepper, and (if desired) salt; cook until onion wilts.

3. Remove skillet from heat. Stir in rice, carrot, cheese, and 1 cup tomato juice; mix well with meat mixture. Spoon filling into peppers. Pour remaining tomato juice into 2-quart baking dish. Stand peppers upright in dish. Cover with foil. Bake until peppers are tender, about 45 minutes. Remove foil; bake 15 additional minutes. To serve, spoon tomato sauce over peppers.

Weekday Beef and Macaroni Skillet

◆ 6 SERVINGS

8 ounces uncooked elbow macaroni, bow ties (farfalle), or other shaped pasta
¾ pound lean ground beef
1 small yellow onion, chopped
1 small green bell pepper, seeds and membranes removed, chopped
8-ounce package fresh mushrooms, wiped clean and sliced
1 garlic clove, chopped
6-ounce can tomato paste
1 cup reduced-sodium beef broth or water
1 teaspoon dried basil or Italian herb seasoning
½ teaspoon hot pepper sauce

1. Cook pasta according to package directions. Meanwhile, in large nonstick skillet, brown beef, onion, and garlic, breaking meat into smaller pieces. Stir in bell pepper and mushrooms. Cook until meat and mushrooms are fully cooked, about 10 minutes.

2. In small bowl, combine tomato paste, broth, basil, and hot pepper sauce; whisk until blended. Stir tomato mixture into beef mixture. Drain macaroni; add to skillet. Stir and toss until well mixed and pasta is coated. Heat through.

You don't have to psyche kids into eating saucy pasta dishes—most go for them naturally. This is healthy fast food. Just add a crisp green salad and call it dinner.

PER SERVING

CALORIES: **316**
PROTEIN: **18 grams**
FAT: **11 grams**
SODIUM: **67 milligrams**
CHOLESTEROL: **35 milligrams**

Saucy Barbecued Beef Sandwiches

Even if I don't watch a football game all season, I get caught up in the Super Bowl super hype. I love planning the menu and having folks over to watch the big game. Television parties are easy to host and a good choice for a novice—just provide an unending stream of great-tasting refreshments, then relax as the tube and your guests provide the entertainment. These savory sandwiches go over well with cheering/jeering fans. Round out your main course with Fireball Vegetable Chili (page 56), Black-eyed Pea Salad (page 59), or Brazilian Black Beans with Marinated Tomatoes (page 58) and baked tortilla chips. Be sure to have lots of paper napkins on hand!

PER SERVING

CALORIES: 347

PROTEIN: 34 grams

FAT: 7 grams

SODIUM: 532 milligrams

CHOLESTEROL: 72 milligrams

◆ 8 SERVINGS

2-pound round steak, about 1 inch thick
Nonstick cooking spray
  1 large yellow onion, chopped
  1 garlic clove, minced
14½-ounce can tomatoes with liquid, cut up
  1 tablespoon Worcestershire sauce
  2 tablespoons apple cider vinegar
  1 tablespoon brown sugar
  1 tablespoon chili powder
  1 teaspoon dried oregano
  1 bay leaf
  8 whole wheat sandwich buns

1. Trim and discard visible fat from meat. To make browning easier, cut meat into 4 pieces. Coat cold dutch oven with nonstick cooking spray. Add half of steak pieces; brown each piece on both sides. Remove browned pieces; add remaining steak and brown. Remove and set aside.

2. Drain all but 1 tablespoon fat from pot. Add onion and garlic; cook and stir about 5 minutes. Stir in remaining ingredients, except buns; mix well.

3. Add browned beef; bring liquid to boil. Reduce heat; simmer until meat is fork-tender, about 2 hours. Remove meat from sauce and transfer to cutting board. Simmer sauce uncovered until slightly thickened, about 5 minutes.

4. Meanwhile, using 2 forks—1 to hold, the other to pull meat apart—shred beef into small pieces. Discard bay leaf. Return meat to sauce; cook just until heated through. Serve beef filling on warmed buns.

Lamb Curry with Sweet Mango Chutney

◆ 8 SERVINGS

1½ pounds boneless lamb
 1 tablespoon vegetable oil
 2 medium-sized yellow onions, chopped
 4 garlic cloves, chopped
 2 tablespoons curry powder
1½ teaspoons salt (optional)
 ⅓ cup raisins
 2 large tomatoes, chopped
 2 fresh green chiles, seeded and minced
 4 cups warm cooked rice
Sweet Mango Chutney (recipe follows)
Optional condiments: chopped apple, banana, nuts, raw
    onion and/or tomatoes; flaked coconut

1. Trim and discard visible fat from lamb; wipe meat with damp paper towels. Cut lamb into 1-inch cubes. In heavy dutch oven, heat vegetable oil; sauté lamb until browned on all sides. Remove lamb from pot and set aside.

2. Pour off and discard all but 1 tablespoon fat from pot. Add onion and garlic; sauté until soft and transparent (do not brown). Stir in curry powder and (if desired) salt until blended. Cook several minutes.

3. Return lamb to pot; stir until meat is coated with curry mixture. Add ½ cup hot water, raisins, tomatoes, and chiles; stir until well mixed. Cover and simmer slowly over low heat, stirring occasionally, until lamb is fork-tender, about 1¼ hours. Skim any fat from surface.

4. Serve over rice. Serve with toppings as desired.

A I prepared for my first trip to Trinidad, I fantasized about a laid-back island of sand and sea. I was surprised to find myself in the midst of a bustling, international city. The fusion of African, Indian, and Chinese cultures produces a multitude of wildly exciting dishes, especially curries. Homemade chutney and other Indian toppings really set this dish off. Serve the condiments in separate bowls so everyone can make their own selections.

PER SERVING WITHOUT CONDIMENTS

CALORIES: 295
PROTEIN: 22 grams
FAT: 7 grams
SODIUM: 55 milligrams
CHOLESTEROL: 58 milligrams

Sweet Mango Chutney

On many Caribbean islands, as in India, a small bowl of chutney is placed on the dinner table to add magical flavor to meals, just as a bottle of hot pepper sauce adorns ours. Most of the chutneys I sampled in Trinidad were made with green mangoes, but the daily-made versions rich with ripe fruit were my favorites. This sweet and tangy chutney makes the ideal counterpoint to spicy curries.

PER TABLESPOON

CALORIES: **36**
PROTEIN: **0 grams**
FAT: **0 grams**
SODIUM: **18 milligrams**
CHOLESTEROL: **0 milligrams**

◆ ABOUT 2½ CUPS

¾ cup white vinegar
½ cup light brown sugar
2 tablespoons finely julienned fresh ginger
1 garlic clove, minced
1 small jalapeño, seeds and membranes removed, minced fine
1 teaspoon grated orange zest
½ teaspoon ground ginger
¼ teaspoon ground allspice
⅛ teaspoon ground turmeric (optional; adds an appealing color)
2 medium-sized ripe yet firm mangoes

1. In medium-sized stainless steel or other nonreactive saucepan, combine vinegar, brown sugar, fresh ginger, garlic, jalapeño, orange zest, ground ginger, allspice, and turmeric. Bring to simmer over medium heat, stirring to dissolve sugar. Cook until syrupy, about 10 minutes.

2. Meanwhile, peel mangoes; cut into ½-inch-thick slices. Cut slices into 1-inch squares. Add mango slices to syrup.

3. Cook, stirring occasionally with wooden spoon, until mangoes are cooked through and coated with heavy syrup, about 20 minutes. If syrup begins to stick, stir in ¼ cup hot water. Let chutney cool to room temperature or chill to serve. Store in glass jar with lid in refrigerator. Will keep in refrigerator 1 week.

Sausage with Kale and Potatoes

◆ 4 SERVINGS

1½ bunches kale

¾ pound reduced-fat kielbasa or other smoked sausage, cut into ¼- to ½-inch-thick rounds

1 large yellow onion, chopped

1 garlic clove, minced

2 large baking potatoes, peeled and sliced ¼ inch thick

2 cups Basic Chicken Broth (page 19), or low-sodium canned chicken broth

1 tablespoon balsamic vinegar

1 teaspoon salt (optional)

½ teaspoon freshly ground black pepper

14½-ounce can whole tomatoes with liquid, chopped

1. Rinse kale in several changes of water; remove and discard stems. Slice or coarsely chop leaves.

2. Place sausage in unheated dutch oven. Over low heat, cook until meat begins to render fat, about 2 minutes. Increase heat to medium; cook until meat is lightly browned around edges. Remove sausage from pot. Pour off all but 1 tablespoon drippings.

3. Add onion, garlic, and potatoes to pot. Cook and stir gently until onion is transparent. Stir in kale; cover and cook about 2 minutes. Return sausage to pot.

4. Stir in broth, vinegar, salt (if desired), and pepper. Bring to boil; reduce heat. Cover and simmer gently 1 hour, stirring in tomatoes during last 30 minutes.

A single pot is all you'll need to cook up this sturdy, down-to-earth stew brimming with old-world flavor.

PER SERVING

CALORIES: **410**

PROTEIN: **20 grams**

FAT: **18 grams**

SODIUM: **241 milligrams**

CHOLESTEROL: **0 milligrams**

The Bread Basket

nlike other forms of cooking, bread-making is part art, part science, and part religious experience. Taking simple grains and transforming them into the "staff of life" can lift us into the realm of the mystical. The satisfaction that comes from baking and eating fresh bread is universal. Since antiquity, societies around the globe have created their signature breads. Here in the States, once again the South gets the nod for the most distinctive tradition. Just-out-of-the-oven biscuits, corn breads, and yeast rolls emit aroma and promise beyond compare.

If you love the notion of rolling up your sleeves and turning on the oven, but feel you don't have the time, let alone the skill, to make bread, you're overestimating what it takes. Most bread baking isn't fussy or demanding. And when you bake your own, you can both reduce the fat and boost the nutritional value. Biscuits and corn bread are excellent choices for beginning bakers. Classified as quick breads, they require no yeast, no kneading, and no preliminary rising for perfect results. Ingredients are few and simple: flour, water, and leavening. Butter makes for tenderness; sweeteners, salt, herbs, and milk add flavor and variations on a theme. Flour or meal is your most important ingredient; select stone-ground for the best quality. Stone grinding (instead of metal rollers) helps retain more of the grain's nutrients and flavor.

Homemade bread also serves as a means of cultural continuity. Sure, we can add hot chiles and shredded cheese to corn bread or chopped pecans and cinnamon to biscuits for more flavor, but at heart, these honest breads do not change, and will continue to tell our stories.

Here perhaps lies a lesson for our day. Sitting down at the table together and "breaking bread"—long a symbol of unity, friendship, and communion—just might solve some of the problems we're facing in our families and in society at large.

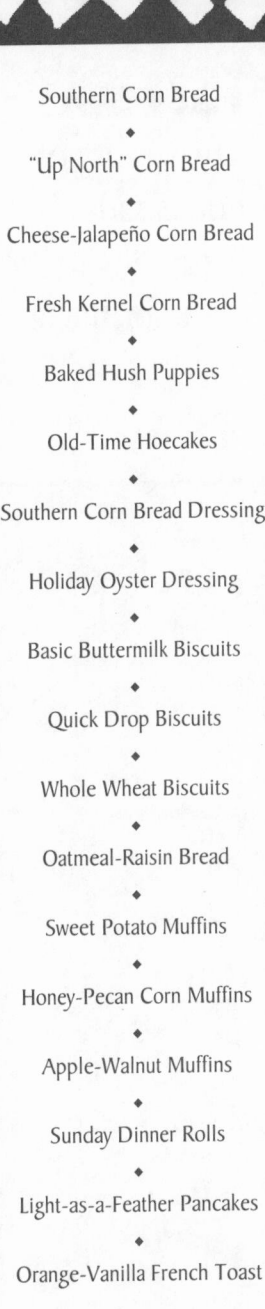

Southern Corn Bread

◆

"Up North" Corn Bread

◆

Cheese-Jalapeño Corn Bread

◆

Fresh Kernel Corn Bread

◆

Baked Hush Puppies

◆

Old-Time Hoecakes

◆

Southern Corn Bread Dressing

◆

Holiday Oyster Dressing

◆

Basic Buttermilk Biscuits

◆

Quick Drop Biscuits

◆

Whole Wheat Biscuits

◆

Oatmeal-Raisin Bread

◆

Sweet Potato Muffins

◆

Honey-Pecan Corn Muffins

◆

Apple-Walnut Muffins

◆

Sunday Dinner Rolls

◆

Light-as-a-Feather Pancakes

◆

Orange-Vanilla French Toast

Fat Chat

The beauty of homemade bread lies in its superior flavor, texture, and health value.

◆ Use a combination of vegetable oil and margarine to replace the solid fat called for in a recipe. The unbiased truth is that solid fats render appealing qualities—tenderness, flakiness, and golden browning—to baked goods. So rather than sacrifice the taste and texture of some breads, compromise can be an acceptable choice.

◆ Replace half of the solid fat in corn bread with half as much nonfat buttermilk or yogurt. For example, in a recipe using 1 cup oil or solid fat, add only ½ cup oil and ¼ cup buttermilk or yogurt. If the batter seems dry, add slightly more of the substitute.

◆ Try whole wheat flour for baking. Because the nutrient-rich bran and germ of whole grains are not refined away, you receive a dose of vitamin E, iron, and natural fiber. Fiber adds needed texture to baked goods made with reduced amounts of fat. Begin by substituting an equal measure of whole wheat flour for up to ⅓ of white flour. (Using a greater proportion of whole wheat flour may require an adjustment to the amount of liquid added.) Like consuming fat, eating dietary fiber produces a feeling of fullness and satisfaction.

◆ Bake in heavy-gauge, nonstick pans. Loaf pans, muffin tins, baking sheets (cookie sheets), griddles, and waffle irons are all available with durable, nonstick finishes.

◆ Avoid overbaking. Using less fat can cause breads to cook more quickly and become dry, so check for doneness before the specified time is up.

◆ Don't stuff that bird. Bake dressing in a separate dish or pan instead of inside the turkey or chicken. This simple step prevents the dressing from soaking up melted fat from the poultry. Even worse than stuffing the bird is placing dressing in the bottom of the roasting pan to cook along with the poultry, as this puts the dressing in contact with an even larger amount of melted fat.

◆ Skim fat from the top of homemade turkey broth before adding to dressing. Discard the fat and use the remaining juices to season and moisten the dressing.

◆ Line muffin cups with paper baking liners. These paper cups prevent muffins from sticking without the usual smear of shortening or butter.

◆ Spread your breakfast muffin or toast with a little all-fruit jam instead of butter. These low-calorie jams add sunny flavors and no fat.

◆ If you must have a little fat with your warm bread, dip it or spread it with olive oil instead of butter. This Mediterranean custom cuts the fat grams by more than half.

HUMBLE CORN BREAD IS TOPS

My mother was a firm believer in "Give us this day our daily bread." On special occasions and some Sundays she would make yeast rolls. All other days, true to her Louisiana heritage, it was her unwavering habit to bake corn bread to go along with dinner. Sometimes she cooked it in a small, six-inch cast-iron skillet on top of the range. Other times, she would spoon the batter into a large skillet and make corn cakes, much the way pancakes are made. And on still other occasions, the batter was baked in a cast-iron mold that made cornsticks shaped like little ears of corn. The methods varied, but never our enjoyment.

Southern Corn Bread

Self-rising cornmeal mix (the cornmeal, flour, leavening, and salt are already combined) has long been a staple in southern cooking. This quick method makes it easy to enjoy fresh-from-the-oven bread even with weekday meals.

PER SERVING

CALORIES: 200
PROTEIN: 5 grams
FAT: 7 grams
SODIUM: 498 milligrams
CHOLESTEROL: 1 milligram

◆ 8 SERVINGS

Nonstick cooking spray
  2 cups self-rising cornmeal mix
1¼ cups skim milk or nonfat buttermilk
  1 whole egg
  1 egg white, slightly beaten
 ¼ cup vegetable oil

1. Heat oven to 425°F. Coat cast-iron skillet with nonstick cooking spray. Place skillet in oven to preheat. Place cornmeal in large mixing bowl; make "well" in center of cornmeal. In medium-sized bowl, mix together milk, egg, egg white, and oil.

2. Add milk mixture all at once to cornmeal, stirring just until moistened (batter should be lumpy). Pour batter into prepared, heated skillet. Bake until golden brown, about 20 to 25 minutes. Serve warm.

"Up North" Corn Bread

◆ 9 SERVINGS

Nonstick cooking spray
  1 cup yellow cornmeal
  1 cup unbleached all-purpose flour
  3 tablespoons sugar
  1 tablespoon plus 1 teaspoon baking powder
  ½ teaspoon salt (optional)
  1 cup skim milk
  ¼ cup vegetable oil
  1 egg, slightly beaten

1. Heat oven to 425°F. Coat 9-inch-square pan with nonstick cooking spray. In medium-sized bowl, combine cornmeal, flour, sugar, baking powder, and (if desired) salt.

2. In small bowl, combine milk, vegetable oil, and egg; mix until blended. Stir liquid mixture into meal mixture; beat by hand just until smooth.

3. Pour batter into prepared pan. Bake until toothpick inserted in center comes out clean, about 20 minutes. Cut into 9 squares.

A distinct line exists between folks who love the no-nonsense character of authentic southern corn bread and those who fancy this yellow, sweeter, less dense relative. Take this basic recipe even farther by stirring in other ingredients, such as sliced scallions, fresh herbs, sun-dried tomatoes, or even by using blue cornmeal. To make muffins, simply spoon the batter into sprayed muffin cups, then bake about 15 minutes. The mini-size muffins are especially nice for brunch, and children love them.

PER SERVING

CALORIES: 192
PROTEIN: 5 grams
FAT: 7 grams
SODIUM: 183 milligrams
CHOLESTEROL: 24 milligrams

Cheese-Jalapeño Corn Bread

The Longhorn State has routinely borrowed ideas and ingredients from the table of their neighbors to the south. This Tex-Mex fusion has produced an array of nationally popular dishes that includes chili, tacos, burritos, and fajitas. Hot chiles that range from mild to incendiary unlock the unique flavors of these dishes. Jalapeños mark the midpoint on the scale that measures the heat generated by peppers. Look for green, shiny jalapeños that feel heavy for their size.

PER SERVING

CALORIES: **129**
PROTEIN: **4 grams**
FAT: **5 grams**
SODIUM: **262 milligrams**
CHOLESTEROL: **31 milligrams**

◆ 16 SERVINGS

1½ cups cornmeal
1 teaspoon baking soda
½ teaspoon salt (optional)
2 large eggs
16-ounce can cream-style corn
1 cup nonfat buttermilk
¼ cup vegetable oil or melted shortening
¾ cup shredded reduced-fat Cheddar cheese or smoked cheese
3 or 4 jalapeño peppers, seeds and membranes removed, sliced thin or chopped fine

1. Heat oven to 350°F. Grease well-seasoned cast-iron 9-inch skillet or baking pan; set aside. In large bowl, mix cornmeal, baking soda, and (if desired) salt. In medium-sized bowl, beat eggs lightly; stir in corn, buttermilk, and shortening until well mixed.

2. Pour liquid mixture into dry ingredients; stir well. Pour half the batter into prepared skillet; sprinkle with half the cheese and half the peppers. Add remaining batter; sprinkle evenly with remaining cheese and peppers. Bake until golden brown and the surface springs back when lightly touched, about 30 to 40 minutes.

Fresh Kernel Corn Bread

◆ 10 SERVINGS

¼ cup vegetable oil
1 cup yellow cornmeal
1 cup unbleached all-purpose flour
1 teaspoon salt (optional)
1 tablespoon plus 1 teaspoon baking powder
1 cup nonfat buttermilk
4 teaspoons honey
1 large egg
1 cup fresh corn kernels (cut from 4 medium-sized ears),
   including "milk" that runs from cob when scraped with
   blunt edge of knife

1. Heat oven to 400°F. Pour oil into seasoned 8-inch cast-iron skillet; rotate to coat bottom and sides. Pour excess oil into small cup; set aside. Place oiled skillet in oven to heat.

2. In large bowl, combine dry ingredients. Add reserved oil, buttermilk, honey, and egg; stir well. Stir in corn with its milk. Pour mixture into hot skillet and bake until corn bread is golden brown, about 20 to 25 minutes. To serve, cut into wedges.

This dense, moist bread delivers a taste sensation similar to that of biting into an ear of newly picked boiled corn on the cob. For the sake of convenience, you might want to make this bread with an 8-ounce can of cream-style corn. The results will be delicious, though not equal to the taste appeal of fresh corn.

PER SERVING

CALORIES: **207**
PROTEIN: **5 grams**
FAT: **7 grams**
SODIUM: **183 milligrams**
CHOLESTEROL: **22 milligrams**

Baked Hush Puppies

In times past, when fishermen and their folks gathered around the fire to fry their catch and swap stories, small fried balls of cornmeal would be tossed to their howling hounds (as the name suggests) to quiet them. This new, baked version resembles mini muffins and is much too good to go to the dogs.

◆ 12 SERVINGS

Nonstick cooking spray
½ cup yellow cornmeal
¼ cup unbleached all-purpose flour
¾ teaspoon baking powder
½ teaspoon granulated sugar
¼ teaspoon salt (optional)
½ teaspoon celery flakes
¼ teaspoon cayenne pepper
1 egg white, beaten
¼ cup skim milk
1 tablespoon vegetable oil
¼ cup finely chopped scallion, including green top

1. Heat oven to 425°F. Using nonstick cooking spray, coat miniature (1¾-inch cups) muffin pan. In medium-sized bowl combine cornmeal, flour, baking powder, sugar, salt (if desired), garlic powder, celery flakes, and cayenne pepper; stir until well blended.

2. In small bowl, combine egg white, milk, and vegetable oil; stir well. Add liquids to dry ingredients; stir just until blended. Stir in scallion. Spoon about 1 tablespoon batter into each muffin cup. Bake until hush puppies are golden brown, about 15 to 20 minutes. Remove immediately; serve warm.

Old-Time Hoecakes

◆ 6 SERVINGS

1½ cups self-rising cornmeal
¼ teaspoon baking soda
1¼ cups nonfat buttermilk
 1 egg, lightly beaten
 2 tablespoons shortening or oil

1. In medium-sized bowl, combine cornmeal and baking soda. Add buttermilk, egg, and 1 tablespoon melted shortening or oil. Stir just until dry ingredients are moistened.

2. Heat remaining 1 tablespoon shortening or oil in heavy, large, nonstick skillet over medium-high heat. Pour ¼ cup batter into skillet for each hoecake. Fry until golden brown on each side, about 1 to 2 minutes per side. Drain on paper towels. Serve immediately.

Take your pick from several accounts of how these quick, savory little breads got their name. One colorful version has it that these flat cakes were the choice of loose women who had neither the time nor inclination to make a proper pan of corn bread. No disrespect to traditional corn bread, but when time is of the essence or you want a thin crusty bread to go along with a hearty soup, hoecakes can't be beat.

PER SERVING

CALORIES: **193**
PROTEIN: **6 grams**
FAT: **6 grams**
SODIUM: **582 milligrams**
CHOLESTEROL: **37 milligrams**

Southern Corn Bread Dressing

The terms STUFFING and DRESSING are often used interchangeably, but to those of us with southern roots, dressing means this well-seasoned dish made with corn bread crumbs. A generous measure of sage is obligatory. The other test of a good dressing is that it is tender and moist, not soggy.

◆ ABOUT 15 SERVINGS

Nonstick cooking spray
¼ cup (½ stick) unsalted butter
1 cup chopped yellow onions
2 cups chopped celery
5 cups crumbled Southern Corn Bread (page 158)
5 cups cubed dry white bread
1 tablespoon salt (optional)
1 teaspoon freshly ground black pepper
1 teaspoon ground thyme
¼ cup chopped parsley
2 teaspoons crumbled dried sage leaves
1 large egg, well beaten
1 egg white, lightly beaten
1½ to 2 cups Basic Chicken Broth (page 19) or turkey broth

1. Heat oven to 375°F. Coat 3-quart baking dish with nonstick cooking spray. Heat butter in heavy saucepan; cook onions and celery until tender but not brown; set aside.

2. In large mixing bowl, blend crumbled corn bread, bread cubes, salt (if desired), black pepper, thyme, parsley, and sage; add onion-celery mixture. Blend in eggs and egg whites; add 1½ cups broth. If mixture seems dry, add another ½ cup broth; stir lightly to blend.

3. Spoon dressing mixture into prepared baking dish. Bake until top is golden brown, about 40 to 45 minutes.

NOTE: The best way to test your uncooked dressing for seasoning is to return a spoonful to the saucepan in which the onion and celery were cooked; cook 3 to 4 minutes. Taste; add more seasoning if desired. In this way you get a much better sample of the finished dish without the risk of eating uncooked eggs.

Holiday Oyster Dressing

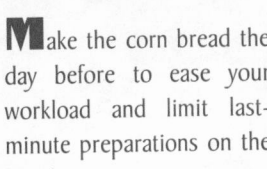

◆ 12 SERVINGS

Nonstick cooking spray
    2 tablespoons butter, margarine, or vegetable oil
    1 cup chopped yellow onions
    1 cup chopped celery
    ½ cup chopped red bell pepper
    2 cups oysters, drained (save liquid)
    ¼ cup chopped parsley
    4 cups crumbled Southern Corn Bread (page 158)
    4 cups cubed stale white or French bread
    1 teaspoon salt (optional)
    ¼ teaspoon ground black pepper
    2 teaspoons poultry seasoning
    1 whole egg, beaten
    1 egg white, beaten
1½ cups Basic Chicken Broth (page 19)
Optional garnish: parsley sprigs

1. Heat oven to 350°F. Coat 9-by-13-inch baking dish with nonstick cooking spray. Melt butter in 6-quart dutch oven over medium heat. Add onions, celery, and bell pepper; sauté until tender, about 5 minutes. Chop oysters; add to vegetables. Cook about 2 minutes; remove from heat.

2. Stir in chopped parsley, corn bread, white bread, salt (if desired), pepper, poultry seasoning, egg and egg white, and broth; mix well. Spoon dressing into prepared casserole dish; bake 45 minutes.

Make the corn bread the day before to ease your workload and limit last-minute preparations on the big day.

PER SERVING

CALORIES: **181**
PROTEIN: **8 grams**
FAT: **8 grams**
SODIUM: **400 milligrams**
CHOLESTEROL: **63 milligrams**

Beautiful Biscuits

Baking biscuits is more joy than chore. But don't become so involved that you overhandle the dough, which makes biscuits tough. Here are more tips for baking better biscuits.

- The dough needs to be kneaded to activate the gluten in the flour. Keep a cool hand and knead gently for just a few seconds.
- Bake on an ungreased or parchment-paper-lined baking sheet in the center of the oven.
- For soft-sided biscuits, arrange them so their sides are almost touching on the baking sheet. For crisper biscuits, space them about 1 inch apart.
- A hot oven (400°F to 450°F) produces a biscuit that's crisp on the outside and moist inside.

Basic Buttermilk Biscuits

◆ ABOUT 18 BISCUITS

2 cups unbleached all-purpose flour
1 tablespoon sugar
2 teaspoons baking powder
¼ teaspoon baking soda
½ teaspoon salt (optional)
⅓ cup solid vegetable shortening
¾ cup nonfat buttermilk

1. Heat oven to 450°F. In large bowl, combine flour, sugar, baking powder, baking soda, and (if desired) salt, using fork to mix well. With pastry blender, cut in shortening until mixture resembles coarse crumbs. Add buttermilk; using fork, mix just until mixture forms soft dough and pulls away from sides of bowl (it may be a bit sticky).

2. Turn dough out onto lightly floured surface; knead 6 to 8 times to mix thoroughly. Roll out dough ½ inch thick. With floured 2-inch round cutter, cut out biscuits.

3. On ungreased baking sheet, place biscuits about 1 inch apart for crusty biscuits, nearly touching for soft-sided biscuits. Press dough scraps together, reroll, and cut until all dough is used. Bake until golden brown, about 12 to 15 minutes.

Flaky, melt-in-your-mouth biscuits are a hallmark of the southern table, so much so that those who made them especially well were held in high regard. Put a napkin-lined basket of warm homemade biscuits on the dinner table and you, too, may bask in the glow of compliments. Biscuits are versatile breads—bake them atop casseroles and savory pies, or top baked biscuits with fresh berries and whipped topping for great shortcakes.

PER BISCUIT

CALORIES: 94
PROTEIN: 2 grams
FAT: 4 grams
SODIUM: 69 milligrams
CHOLESTEROL: 0 milligrams

Quick Drop Biscuits

These are the biscuits of choice for people in a hurry or those who favor a crusty outside.

◆ 12 BISCUITS

Nonstick cooking spray
2 cups self-rising flour
¼ cup vegetable shortening
About 1 cup skim or 1-percent-fat milk

1. Heat oven to 475°F. Coat baking sheet with nonstick cooking spray.

2. Place flour in mixing bowl and cut in shortening with pastry blender or fork until mixture resembles coarse crumbs. Using fork, blend in just enough milk so dough pulls away from sides of bowl.

3. Turn dough onto lightly floured surface. Knead gently 10 to 12 strokes. Drop from tablespoon onto prepared baking sheet. Bake 8 to 10 minutes.

Whole Wheat Biscuits

◆ 12 BISCUITS

1 cup whole wheat flour
1 cup unbleached all-purpose flour
1 tablespoon sugar
1 tablespoon plus 1 teaspoon baking powder
1 teaspoon salt (optional)
¼ cup vegetable shortening
1 cup skim milk

1. Heat oven to 450°F. In large mixing bowl, combine whole wheat flour, all-purpose flour, sugar, baking powder, and (if desired) salt; mix well. Cut in shortening until mixture resembles coarse crumbs. Add milk gradually, stirring until dough forms.

2. Turn out onto lightly floured surface; knead slightly. Roll dough to ½-inch thickness; using 2½-inch cookie cutter dipped in flour, cut straight down to cut out biscuits. Arrange on ungreased baking sheet. Bake until golden-toned, about 12 to 15 minutes.

This is the recipe you've been looking for—biscuits that are wholesome, nutty-flavored, and slightly sweet. Enjoy them right out of the oven with jam and a cup of herb tea.

PER BISCUIT

CALORIES: **128**
PROTEIN: **3 grams**
FAT: **5 grams**
SODIUM: **132 milligrams**
CHOLESTEROL: **0 milligrams**

Oatmeal-Raisin Bread

Oats and raisins have a natural affinity. This bread is delicious with eggs and sausage and makes wonderful toast. Molasses adds rich, deep color and taste.

◆ I LOAF; 10 SERVINGS

Nonstick cooking spray
 I cup rolled oats (regular or quick-cooking)
 I cup unbleached all-purpose flour
 I teaspoon baking soda
 I½ teaspoons baking powder
 ½ teaspoon salt (optional)
 ½ cup raisins
 I teaspoon grated lemon zest
 ½ teaspoon ground cinnamon
 ¼ teaspoon grated nutmeg
 I egg, slightly beaten
 2 tablespoons molasses
 I cup nonfat buttermilk
 2 tablespoons vegetable oil
Optional garnish: I tablespoon rolled oats

1. Heat oven to 350°F. Using nonstick cooking spray, coat 9-by-5-inch loaf pan; set aside. In large bowl, combine oats, flour, baking soda, baking powder, salt (if desired), raisins, zest, cinnamon, and nutmeg.

2. In medium-sized bowl, combine egg, molasses, buttermilk, and vegetable oil; stir to mix well. Pour into dry mixture; stir until blended.

3. Spoon batter into prepared pan; sprinkle with I tablespoon rolled oats. Bake until wooden pick inserted in center comes out clean, about 50 minutes. Cool in pan 10 minutes; turn bread out onto cooling rack. Serve warm or cool.

Sweet Potato Muffins

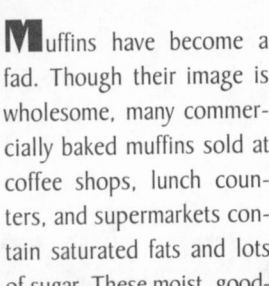

◆ 18 MUFFINS

Nonstick cooking spray
1½ cups unbleached all-purpose flour
½ cup granulated sugar
½ cup packed brown sugar
2 teaspoons baking powder
1 teaspoon ground cinnamon
¼ teaspoon ground nutmeg
¼ teaspoon salt (optional)
1 cup mashed cooked sweet potatoes (home-cooked or canned)
1 whole egg
1 egg white
2 tablespoons vegetable oil
½ cup raisins
Optional topping: Sprinkle mixture of 2 tablespoons sugar and ¼ teaspoon ground cinnamon over tops of muffins BEFORE baking

Muffins have become a fad. Though their image is wholesome, many commercially baked muffins sold at coffee shops, lunch counters, and supermarkets contain saturated fats and lots of sugar. These moist, good-for-you breads are a taste treat.

PER MUFFIN
CALORIES: **135**
PROTEIN: **2 grams**
FAT: **2 grams**
SODIUM: **52 milligrams**
CHOLESTEROL: **12 milligrams**

1. Heat oven to 375°F. Coat 18 (2½-inch) muffin cups with cooking spray, or line with paper liners. In large bowl, using fork, combine flour, granulated sugar, brown sugar, baking powder, cinnamon, nutmeg, and (if desired) salt; mix until blended.

2. In small bowl, combine sweet potatoes, egg, egg white, and vegetable oil; stir until mixed. Add sweet potato mixture all at once to flour mixture. Using spoon, stir just until combined. Stir in raisins.

3. Spoon batter evenly into muffin cups, filling each ¾ full. Bake until wooden pick inserted into center of muffin comes out clean, about 20 minutes. Remove muffins from tin; serve warm.

Honey-Pecan Corn Muffins

Take a basket of these muffins to the family re-union picnic and brighten everyone's day.

PER MUFFIN

CALORIES: **257**
PROTEIN: **4 grams**
FAT: **13 grams**
SODIUM: **136 milligrams**
CHOLESTEROL: **19 milligrams**

◆ 12 MUFFINS

Nonstick cooking spray
1¼ cups yellow cornmeal
  1 cup unbleached all-purpose flour
  ¼ cup packed brown sugar
  1 teaspoon baking soda
  ½ teaspoon ground cinnamon (optional)
  ½ teaspoon salt (optional)
  1 large egg
  1 cup nonfat buttermilk
  ½ cup vegetable oil
  ¼ cup honey
  ½ cup coarsely chopped pecans

1. Heat oven to 400°F. Using cooking spray, coat 12 (2½-inch) muffin cups or 36 miniature cups. In large mixing bowl, using fork, mix cornmeal, flour, brown sugar, baking soda, and (if desired) cinnamon and salt.

2. In small bowl, using fork, beat egg slightly; then stir in buttermilk, oil, and honey. Add egg mixture and pecans all at once to flour mixture. Using spoon, stir just until dry ingredients are moistened; batter should be lumpy.

3. Spoon batter into prepared muffin cups. Bake until muffins are golden brown and wooden pick inserted in center comes out clean and dry, about 20 to 25 minutes. Turn muffins from pan onto wire rack; serve at once, or keep warm by leaving in cups. (If you leave them in pan, tilt muffins in cups to allow steam to escape and prevent soggy bottoms.)

Apple-Walnut Muffins

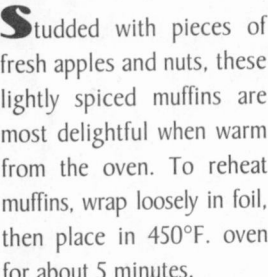

Studded with pieces of fresh apples and nuts, these lightly spiced muffins are most delightful when warm from the oven. To reheat muffins, wrap loosely in foil, then place in 450°F. oven for about 5 minutes.

◆ 12 TO 16 MUFFINS

Nonstick cooking spray
- ½ cup margarine
- ½ cup packed light brown sugar
- 2 large eggs
- 2 cups unbleached all-purpose flour
- ½ teaspoon salt (optional)
- 2 tablespoons baking powder
- 1 teaspoon ground cinnamon
- ½ cup skim milk or 1-percent-fat milk
- 2½ cups peeled, chopped apples
- ½ cup chopped walnuts

Optional topping: granulated or brown sugar

PER MUFFIN

CALORIES: 210
PROTEIN: 5 grams
FAT: 10 grams
SODIUM: 248 milligrams
CHOLESTEROL: 31 milligrams

1. Heat oven to 375°F. Coat 12 to 16 (2½-inch) muffin-tin cups with nonstick cooking spray or line with paper liners. In large bowl, cream margarine and sugar. Add eggs one at a time, beating well. Sift dry ingredients together; add to egg mixture alternately with milk. Beat until smooth. Stir in apples and nuts.

2. Spoon batter into prepared muffin tins until ¾ full; sprinkle with sugar. Bake 25 to 30 minutes.

Sunday Dinner Rolls

Mother's homemade yeast rolls always graced our celebration table. Though the main attraction of the big dinner might be a glazed Smithfield ham, an over-stuffed turkey, or English-cut beef roast, the rolls always drew praise. I guess that's why she was so disappointed when I didn't include this recipe in my first cookbook. Although the book featured over 300 recipes, Moms felt it was one recipe short and never failed to mention it when the subject of my book came up. So including it here will make her happy, and if you make them, I'm sure you will be quite pleased, too.

PER ROLL

CALORIES: **147**
PROTEIN: **4 grams**
FAT: **4 grams**
SODIUM: **18 milligrams**
CHOLESTEROL: **15 milligrams**

◆ ABOUT 2½ DOZEN ROLLS

 1 cup 1-percent-fat milk, scalded
½ cup granulated sugar
 2 teaspoons salt (optional)
½ cup vegetable shortening, margarine, or butter
 2 packets active dry yeast
 1 cup evaporated skim milk
 2 large eggs, slightly beaten
 5 to 6 cups unbleached all-purpose flour

1. In medium bowl mix scalded milk, sugar, salt (if desired), and shortening; stir until sugar dissolves. Let cool to lukewarm.

2. Pour ½ cup lukewarm water into large warm bowl; sprinkle in yeast; stir until dissolved. Stir in milk mixture, evaporated milk, eggs, and about 2 cups flour; beat with wooden spoon until smooth. Mix in enough additional flour, a little at a time, to make a soft dough. It will be sticky but should leave sides of bowl.

3. Turn out onto lightly floured surface; knead 6 to 8 minutes until smooth and elastic. Shape into large ball. Place in large greased bowl; turn dough to grease all over. Cover with clean cloth and let rise in warm, draft-free spot until doubled in size, about 30 to 40 minutes.

4. Punch dough down by shoving your fist deep into its center (it will collapse). Shape dough into 2-inch round balls and arrange on greased baking pans; cover and let rise about ½ hour until doubled in size.

5. About 15 minutes before baking, preheat oven to 375°F. Bake rolls until golden brown and one sounds hollow when tapped, about 15 to 20 minutes.

Light-as-a-Feather Pancakes

◆ 16 (4-INCH) PANCAKES

    2 egg whites
    2 cups nonfat buttermilk
    3 tablespoons vegetable oil
1¾ cups unbleached all-purpose flour
    2 tablespoons granulated sugar
    2 teaspoons baking powder
    1 teaspoon baking soda
 ¼ teaspoon salt (optional)

1. Heat griddle or large skillet to medium-high heat (400°F.). In large bowl, beat egg whites until foamy; stir in buttermilk and vegetable oil. Add remaining ingredients; stir just until large lumps disappear. (For thinner pancakes, thin with additional milk.)

2. Lightly grease heated griddle; a few drops of water sprinkled on griddle will sizzle and bounce when heat is just right. Pour batter, about ¼ cup at a time, onto hot griddle. Bake until bubbles form on top and edges start to dry; turn and bake other side. (Turn only once.)

Variations:

APPLE PANCAKES: Add ½ cup peeled, shredded apple and ½ teaspoon cinnamon to the batter.

BANANA PANCAKES: Add 1 cup mashed ripe bananas to batter.

NUT PANCAKES: Add ½ cup chopped nuts to batter.

WHOLE WHEAT PANCAKES: Use 1 cup all-purpose flour and ¾ cup whole wheat flour.

TIP: To prepare pancakes using skim or 1-percent-fat milk, decrease milk to 1¾ cups, increase baking powder to 4 teaspoons, and omit baking soda.

What a sunny way to start the day! These tender, moist cakes allow us to continue enjoying a childhood favorite. Measure and mix dry ingredients the night before to jump-start breakfast preparation. Be creative and come up with your own variations.

PER BASIC PANCAKE

CALORIES: **96**
PROTEIN: **3 grams**
FAT: **3 grams**
SODIUM: **163 milligrams**
CHOLESTEROL: **1 milligram**

Orange-Vanilla French Toast

Refrigerate batter-dipped bread overnight to cook quickly the next morning. On those cold, wintery, weekend mornings, plan to hop back in bed and enjoy a warm, nourishing breakfast in the sack. Instead of syrup, pour fresh fruit purée (process in blender or food processor) over toast for a healthful topping.

PER TOAST SLICE

CALORIES: **325**
PROTEIN: **15 grams**
FAT: **11 grams**
SODIUM: **482 milligrams**
CHOLESTEROL: **110 milligrams**

◆ 8 SLICES TOAST; 4 SERVINGS

    2 whole eggs
    2 egg whites
  ¾ cup skim milk, or 1-percent-fat milk
  ¼ cup orange juice
    1 tablespoon granulated sugar or honey
    1 teaspoon grated orange zest (optional)
    1 teaspoon ground cinnamon
  ½ teaspoon pure vanilla extract
    8 slices whole wheat or white bread
    2 tablespoons margarine
8-ounce container low-fat vanilla yogurt
Optional garnish: orange slices

1. In large shallow bowl or pie plate, using fork, beat eggs and egg whites lightly. Stir in milk, orange juice, sugar (if desired), orange zest, ½ teaspoon cinnamon, and vanilla. Dip both sides of each slice of bread into batter.

2. On griddle or in large skillet, melt 1 tablespoon margarine; spread evenly over surface to coat. Add several bread slices and cook over medium heat until lightly browned; turn each and brown other side. Remove to warm platter or keep warm in 200°F. oven. Add remaining margarine to skillet as needed, and pan-fry remaining bread slices in batches. Spoon yogurt over toast; sprinkle with remaining ½ teaspoon cinnamon. Serve warm; garnish with orange slices.

Sweet Seduction: Guilt-free Desserts

As a child, sitting on a hard church pew each Sunday with my family, I often envisioned the road to heaven paved with peach cobbler, coconut layer cake, and sweet potato pie. Sold whole or by the slice, these mouth-watering desserts adorned the bake-sale table most Sundays. The good sisters of the church would bring in their home-baked treasures and set up shop just before the service ended. I could hardly wait to get to the basement to see their display. I had seen perfect-looking cakes and pies in bakeries, but none looked as delicious as these. For a moment I felt guilty buying a slice of Mrs. Tucker's pie with the quarter given me to drop in the collection plate. But after the first taste, I was happy with the thought that the money had still gone to the church.

Now you can drop the guilt of indulgence and dive into low-fat but luscious pineapple upside-down cake, heavenly sweet potato pie, and bread pudding with tipsy raisin sauce, all featured in this chapter. Ours is a sweet legacy and now those time-honored desserts can be made without butter, oil, whole eggs, or excess sugar.

There are plenty of fat-free store-bought desserts on the market these days, but my gripe with many of them is that when they remove the fat, they add a ton of sugar, which means that while these desserts may not have a single gram of fat, they are still high in calories and excess calories turn into fat. The fat-conscious treasures in this chapter rely instead on an extra dash of spice, a splash of flavoring extract, or fresh, ripe fruit.

Since desserts should delight, show them off: Take out the milk-glass cake stand, colored Depression-glass plates, etched parfait glasses, silver pie server, or other heirlooms or garage-sale finds waiting in your china cabinet. Add non-sprayed lemon leaves, fresh mint, julienned citrus peel, or long-stemmed strawberries to dress them for the occasion.

A bonus blessing: Scrumptious, low-fat desserts made from wholesome ingredients not only satisfy your sweet tooth but also help meet your body's daily requirements for an array of important vitamins and minerals. And you thought they just tasted great.

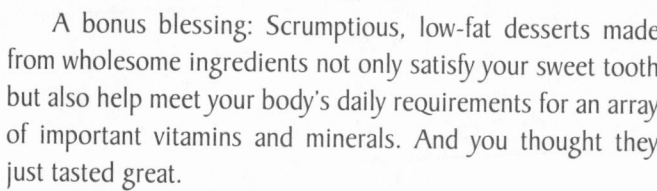

Fat Chat
Your hips never have to know you've had dessert!

◆ Revel in the naturally sweet, juicy flavors of fresh fruit. Stay with the seasons—blueberries in May, cherries in June, watermelon in July—for peak flavor and valley prices. Fructose, the natural sugar in fruit, is a healthier choice than refined white sugar.

◆ Select no-fat and low-fat dairy products. Milk, buttermilk, evaporated milk, sweetened condensed milk, yogurt, cream cheese, and sour cream are all available in reduced-fat versions. Evaporated skim milk (commonly known as "canned milk") is a great deceiver when it comes to adding creamy texture to pies, cakes, and other baked goods.

◆ Make fruit pies with just a single crust. Open-face pies and tarts (crust on bottom) show off the beauty of fresh fruit. Or place fruit filling directly in the pie plate and top with a lattice or standard piecrust.

◆ Substitute, substitute, substitute! Applesauce, prune purée (jarred baby food is easy to use), mashed bananas, or yogurt can be used in place of half or more the fat in cakes, cookies, and brownies. Try raisins in place of chocolate chips.

◆ Instead of high-fat frosting, simply dust a cake with confectioners' sugar.

◆ Chocolate lovers, use cocoa powder instead of chocolate. Cocoa offers the same enchanting taste without the saturated fat. Replace each ounce of baking chocolate in cakes, brownies, and other desserts with 2 teaspoons water added to 3 tablespoons cocoa powder and save 13.5 grams fat and III calories!

◆ Whip chilled evaporated skim milk instead of cream for a dreamy nonfat topping. Simple fruit cups, pies, puddings, short cakes, and cakes become showcase desserts with just an added dollop. The milk, bowl, and mixer must be well chilled for best results; serve right away.

Tropical Ambrosia

Ambrosia—what a romantic inspiration. The word rolls off the tongue like the name of a beautiful woman or a fresh breeze on shore after the rain. A glass bowl with straight sides shows off the gemlike colors of this layered fruit salad. Toast almonds to enhance nutty flavor. Serve as a first course for brunch or as a light dessert following a luncheon or heavy meal.

PER SERVING

CALORIES: 253
PROTEIN: 3 grams
FAT: 5 grams
SODIUM: 15 milligrams
CHOLESTEROL: 0 milligrams

◆ 8 SERVINGS

 2 ripe yet firm bananas, sliced into rounds
Juice of 1 lemon (about 2 tablespoons)
 ¼ cup confectioners' sugar
 ½ cup sweetened flaked coconut
 2 large navel oranges, peeled, pith and seeds removed, sliced crosswise into pinwheels
 2 cups fresh pineapple chunks, or canned pineapple packed in juice
 2 large ripe papayas, peeled, seeded, and sliced crosswise
 2 large kiwifruit, peeled and sliced
 ½ cup slivered almonds (plain or toasted)
 ¼ cup pineapple or orange juice
 1 teaspoon coconut extract

1. In small bowl, sprinkle bananas with lemon juice; toss to coat bananas to prevent browning. In glass serving bowl, arrange bananas as bottom layer; sprinkle lightly with about ⅕ confectioners' sugar and coconut.

2. Repeat same procedure with layers of oranges, pineapple, papayas, and kiwifruit. Combine fruit juice and extract; drizzle over fruit. Sprinkle top with almonds. Cover bowl with plastic wrap and refrigerate until chilled and juicy, about 1 hour or until serving time (up to about 5 hours).

NOTE: To toast nuts, spread in single layer on baking sheet. Bake at 350°F until light golden and fragrant, about 10 minutes. Do not overbake.

Fruit Salad in Watermelon Bowl

◆ 20 SERVINGS

1 (9-pound) oval-shaped watermelon
1 pint fresh blueberries
2 ripe yet firm bananas, sliced into rounds, tossed with fresh lemon juice
1 honeydew melon, halved, seeded, rind removed, cut into chunks or scooped into balls
1 large ripe pineapple, peeled, cored, cut into bite-sized chunks or three 16-ounce cans pineapple chunks packed in juice
1 pound seedless red, green, or black grapes, seeds removed
2 navel oranges, peeled and cut into quarters, sliced ½ inch thick
¼ cup chopped candied ginger (optional)
¼ cup orange juice
¼ cup fruit-flavored liqueur of choice (such as Cointreau, Grand Marnier, Cherry Heering, Calvados, or Midori)
Optional garnish: whole or sliced fresh mint leaves

A carved watermelon overflowing with a colorful mélange of fresh fruit makes an eye-catching, light-hearted dessert for outdoor summer gatherings. For a delightful surprise, select a yellow-fleshed watermelon. This recipe makes about 20 servings; for a smaller group, cut this recipe down to size and present it in a mini-sized Sweet Baby watermelon.

PER SERVING

CALORIES: **109**
PROTEIN: **1 gram**
FAT: **1 gram**
SODIUM: **8 milligrams**
CHOLESTEROL: **0 milligrams**

1. To carve watermelon bowl: Using long, sharp knife, make lengthwise cut about 3 inches from top of watermelon; remove top. Scoop out red pulp in large pieces and place in large bowl; drain juice from melon into bowl. Cut thin slice of rind from watermelon bottom so it sits level. Using short, sharp knife, score an even scallop or sawtooth pattern around top rim of shell, then cut out etched pattern. Cover top with plastic wrap; refrigerate until serving time.

2. Remove and discard seeds from watermelon pulp. Cut into chunks or carve into balls. Return watermelon pieces to large bowl; add remaining fruit and ginger. Drizzle with orange juice and liqueur; toss gently to coat. Empty fruit salad into watermelon bowl.

Fresh Peach Cobbler

This biscuit-style crust distinguishes cobblers from other deep-dish fruit pies, and sweet, ripe peaches make this a height-of-summer delight. For you four-season fans I'm including a desperation version, so you can use canned peaches when fresh are not at their best, or no longer around.

PER SERVING

CALORIES: **200**
PROTEIN: **3 grams**
FAT: **4 grams**
SODIUM: **39 milligrams**
CHOLESTEROL: **0 milligrams**

◆ 10 SERVINGS

Crust:

- 1 cup unbleached all-purpose flour
- 1½ teaspoons baking powder
- ¼ teaspoon salt (optional)
- 2 tablespoons granulated sugar
- 3 tablespoons vegetable shortening or butter or cream cheese, chilled
- 3 to 4 tablespoons 1-percent-fat milk

Filling:

- 8 cups sliced, fully ripe peaches (about 12 medium-sized peaches)
- 1 tablespoon fresh lemon juice
- ½ cup granulated sugar
- 2 tablespoons cornstarch
- 1 teaspoon ground cinnamon
- ½ teaspoon ground nutmeg
- 1 teaspoon pure vanilla extract

Nonstick cooking spray

1. To make crust: In large bowl, stir together flour, baking powder, salt (if desired), and 1 tablespoon sugar. Cut in shortening until mixture resembles coarse meal. Sprinkle milk over mixture; stir with fork until dough forms ball. Knead 4 or 5 times; wrap in plastic wrap and chill at least 1 hour.

2. Meanwhile, to prepare filling: In large bowl, combine peaches and lemon juice; toss to coat peaches. In small bowl combine the ½ cup sugar, cornstarch, cinnamon, and nutmeg. Sprinkle peaches with sugar mixture and vanilla; toss to coat peaches.

3. Heat oven to 400°F. On lightly floured surface, roll dough into 12-by-8-inch rectangle. Spoon peach filling into 12-by-8-inch baking dish coated with nonstick cooking spray. Arrange dough over peaches; sprinkle with 1 tablespoon sugar reserved from crust. Bake until syrup bubbles around edges of dish and crust is golden brown, about 35 minutes.

NOTE: To make with canned peaches, use six 1-pound cans of peaches packed in juice (instead of syrup). Decrease sugar in recipe by half.

Lemon Icebox Pie in Almond Crust

My aunt Mary was never much for cooking. She preferred the easy way out of the kitchen and would pop open canned vegetables and other convenience foods instead of fresh. She had one dish, however, that we all swooned over—her icebox pie. This updated version uses the new fat-free condensed milk and lots of freshly squeezed lemon juice. The additional step of baking before chilling guards against the risk of eating uncooked egg yolks. A nutty crust sets off the citrus flavor deliciously. Keep slices thin; the flavor is intense!

PER SERVING

CALORIES: **223**
PROTEIN: **6 grams**
FAT: **8 grams**
SODIUM: **142 milligrams**
CHOLESTEROL: **77 milligrams**

◆ ONE 8-INCH PIE; 10 SERVINGS

Almond Crust:

1 cup finely crushed graham cracker crumbs or vanilla wafers
⅓ cup (2 ounces) finely chopped almonds
1 tablespoon sugar
½ teaspoon almond or vanilla extract
2 tablespoons butter, melted

Filling:

3 large egg yolks
14-ounce can low-fat or fat-free sweetened condensed milk (not evaporated milk)
½ cup freshly squeezed lemon juice (about 3 medium-sized lemons)
Optional garnish: lemon leaves. (If using leaves from florist—which likely have been sprayed with insecticide—do not put in contact with food; use only around outside of pie plate.)

1. To make crust: Measure crumbs into medium-sized bowl; add almonds, sugar, and butter. Stir and toss until well mixed. Very lightly butter or spray 8-inch pie plate; add crust mixture. Pour crust mixture into 8-inch pie plate; using back of spoon, press mixture onto bottom and sides of plate, making small rim.

2. Position rack in center of oven; heat to 350°F.

3. To prepare filling: In medium-sized bowl, beat egg yolks with condensed milk and lemon juice. Pour into prepared crust; spread evenly. Sprinkle with reserved crumb mixture, if you chose to reserve. Bake 30 minutes. Let cool; refrigerate until chilled and time to serve. Refrigerate leftovers.

Banana Cream Pie

◆ ONE 9-INCH PIE; 8 SERVINGS

9-inch baked Basic Piecrust (page 189)
 3 tablespoons cornstarch
14-ounce can low-fat sweetened condensed milk
    (not evaporated milk)
 2 egg yolks, beaten
 1 tablespoon dark rum
 1 teaspoon pure vanilla extract
 2 tablespoons fresh lemon juice
 1 tablespoon honey
 3 ripe yet firm medium-sized bananas

1. Prepare piecrust and set aside. In heavy-bottomed saucepan, dissolve cornstarch in 1 cup water. Stir in sweetened condensed milk and egg yolks. Cook and stir until thickened and bubbly, about two minutes. Remove from heat; stir in rum and vanilla. Let cool slightly.

2. Meanwhile, in medium-sized bowl, blend lemon juice and honey. Slice bananas into honey-lemon mixture. Toss to coat bananas; drain juice, if any. Arrange half of banana slices on bottom of piecrust.

3. Carefully pour custard over bananas; even and smooth top. Arrange remaining banana slices in overlapping circle around edge of custard. Cover with plastic wrap. Chill until set, about 4 hours. Refrigerate any leftovers.

A hint of rum livens up the flavor of this traditional southern favorite. Try red-skinned bananas for a sweet and creamy difference.

PER SERVING

CALORIES: 324
PROTEIN: 7 grams
FAT: 9 grams
SODIUM: 149 milligrams
CHOLESTEROL: 70 milligrams

Heavenly Sweet Potato Pie

It's a toss-up as to which of several southern classic desserts would place second, but sweet-potato pie has to be the all-time number-one favorite. Instead of boiling the potatoes, sometimes I bake them until tender. Baking seems to bring out more of the potato's natural sweetness and does not leach out nutrients as boiling tends to do.

◆ ONE 9-INCH PIE; 8 SERVINGS

4 medium-sized sweet potatoes
½ cup granulated sugar
1 teaspoon ground cinnamon
½ teaspoon ground ginger
½ teaspoon ground nutmeg
1½ cups evaporated skim milk (12-ounce can)
1 teaspoon pure vanilla extract
1 teaspoon grated orange zest
3 egg whites, lightly beaten
¼ cup brandy
9-inch unbaked Basic Piecrust (page 189)

1. PREPARE POTATOES: To BAKE, prick potatoes in several places and bake in 425°F oven until soft, about 45 minutes. To BOIL, place sweet potatoes and enough cold water to cover in large saucepan. Partially cover with lid; set over high heat and bring to boil. Reduce heat; simmer potatoes until fork-tender, about 45 minutes; drain potatoes.

2. If potatoes were boiled, heat oven to 425°F. When cool enough to handle, peel potatoes and remove blemishes. Mash potatoes in large bowl, using potato masher or fork. (To remove lumps or strings, use food mill or press potatoes through standard sieve back into bowl.)

3. In small bowl, combine sugar, cinnamon, ginger, and nutmeg; mix well. Stir spice mixture into mashed sweet potatoes until blended. Add vanilla, milk, and orange zest; fold in egg whites. Using electric mixer, beat until smooth; stir in brandy.

4. Pour filling into unbaked pie crust; bake 10 minutes. Reduce heat to 325°F; bake until knife inserted in filling comes out clean, about 45 additional minutes. Serve warm or chilled. Cover and refrigerate any leftovers.

Basic Piecrust

◆ 1 9-INCH PIECRUST

1 cup unbleached all-purpose flour

⅛ teaspoon salt (optional)

¼ cup (½ stick) vegetable shortening or margarine made from polyunsaturated oil

4 to 5 tablespoons ice water

1. In large bowl, combine flour and (if desired) salt. Using pastry blender or two knives, cut shortening lightly into flour until mixture resembles coarse meal. Add 5 to 7 tablespoons ice water a few tablespoons at a time; mix lightly and quickly until pastry forms ball. Flatten into circle about 1 inch thick. Wrap with waxed paper; refrigerate at least 1 hour (or up to 2 days).

2. To roll out dough, place between 12-inch-square sheets of waxed paper. Let dough soften slightly, about 5 minutes (dough should remain chilled). Roll dough from center to edges, forming a 12-inch circle about ⅛ inch thick. Or place dough on lightly floured surface, sprinkle top with small amount of flour, then roll out with lightly floured rolling pin.

3. To line pie pan, remove top layer of waxed paper. Invert dough into pan and peel away other sheet of waxed paper. Center dough; press it lightly into pan with your fingertips. Trim dough evenly so it hangs about 1 inch past outer edge of pan. Fold edges of the dough under itself; flute. Chill about 30 minutes before filling or baking.

4. For baked pie shell (to be filled later), heat oven to 400°F. To cook partially, bake 8 to 10 minutes. For fully baked crust, remove when edges are light brown, about 10 to 15 minutes. To keep unfilled piecrust from shrinking or puffing during baking, line with aluminum foil, then add dried beans as alternative to metal or ceramic weights. Keep these beans on hand for reuse; store in container separate from edible beans.

In addition to desserts, use this pastry crust for main-dish pot pies, meat or vegetable turnovers, or quiches. For a whole wheat crust, substitute half or more whole wheat pastry flour for the all-purpose flour. If using all whole wheat flour, add 1 teaspoon baking powder along with the salt to lighten the texture.

PER SERVING

CALORIES: 111
PROTEIN: 2 grams
FAT: 6 grams
SODIUM: 67 milligrams
CHOLESTEROL: 0 milligrams

Maple Baked Apples

When the air is refreshingly crisp and leaves turn golden, this easy-to-make dessert brings an autumn brunch or dinner to a homey end. Select Cortland, Rome Beauty, or other large red baking apples. These are delicious served with low-fat vanilla ice cream or whipped topping.

The Algonquins, one of the Native American tribes that settled in the Northeast, introduced the early colonists to tapping maple trees and collecting the sweet sap. Pure maple syrup and ground spices contribute to this dessert's naturally irresistible flavor.

PER SERVING
CALORIES: **203**
PROTEIN: **1 gram**
FAT: **1 gram**
SODIUM: **8 milligrams**
CHOLESTEROL: **0 milligrams**

◆ 6 SERVINGS

6 large Rome Beauty or other crisp red cooking apples
Juice of 1 lemon (about 2 tablespoons)
¼ cup raisins
1 teaspoon grated lemon zest
¼ cup pure maple syrup
1 teaspoon ground cinnamon
½ teaspoon freshly grated nutmeg
1½ cups apple juice

1. Heat oven to 375°F. Using apple corer or sharp paring knife, core each apple to 1 inch above bottom. Spoon equal amounts of lemon juice into each "well."

2. In small bowl, mix raisins, lemon zest, and ⅛ cup maple syrup; spoon an equal amount into each apple cavity. Arrange apples in baking dish. Drizzle remaining ⅛ cup syrup over the apples; sprinkle with cinnamon and nutmeg. Pour apple juice into dish.

3. Cover baking dish loosely with aluminum foil; bake until apples are tender when pierced with toothpick, about 1 hour and 15 minutes. Serve hot or at room temperature.

Fat-free Angel Food Cake

◆ 14 SERVINGS

1 cup sifted cake flour

1¼ cups confectioners' sugar

12 egg whites from large eggs, at room temperature

1½ teaspoons cream of tartar

½ teaspoon pure vanilla extract

¼ teaspoon almond extract

½ cup granulated sugar

Optional garnishes: Whipped Dessert Topping (page 204), fresh berries, sliced fresh fruit

This light sponge cake is wonderfully guilt-free. It has no butter, shortening, or other fat added. The secret is egg whites beaten to a great volume. Slather slices with whipped topping and fresh seasonal fruit (strawberries are superb) or Tropical Ambrosia (page 182).

PER SERVING

CALORIES: 114
PROTEIN: 4 grams
FAT: 0 grams
SODIUM: 48 milligrams
CHOLESTEROL: 0 milligrams

1. Heat oven to 375°F. Into large bowl, sift together flour and confectioners' sugar. Place egg whites in medium-sized, deep bowl of standing electric mixer or in mixing bowl. Using standing or portable mixer on low speed, beat egg whites until foamy, about 1 minute.

2. Add cream of tartar and extracts. Gradually increase mixer speed to high. While beating, sprinkle in granulated sugar, about 2 tablespoons at a time. When all sugar has been added, use rubber spatula to scrape sides and bottom of bowl. Resume beating at high speed until egg whites are stiff but moist.

3. To fold flour mixture into whites, sift approximately ⅓ of flour-sugar mixture over top of egg whites. Using rubber spatula, cut through to bottom of bowl and lift egg whites up and over flour; continue until all flour has been folded in. Repeat, adding ⅓ of flour mixture at a time.

4. Pour batter into ungreased 10-inch tube pan very carefully (so batter will not begin to deflate). Cut through batter several times to burst any large air bubbles. Smooth top with rubber spatula. Place pan on middle rack in oven. Bake until top of cake springs back when touched lightly with finger, about 40 to 50 minutes.

5. Remove cake from oven and immediately turn upside down onto feet of tube pan. (If pan has no feet, place bottle or funnel in center of tube pan and stand on bottle.) Let stand until pan is no longer warm. Insert thin spatula between edges of cake and pan, loosening cake. Remove to cake plate.

Healthy Carrot Cake

◆ 12 SERVINGS

Nonstick cooking spray
- 2 cups light brown sugar
- ½ cup applesauce
- ½ cup low-fat buttermilk
- ¼ cup honey
- 2 eggs
- 1 egg white
- 2 cups flour
- 1½ teaspoons cinnamon
- ½ teaspoon salt (optional)
- 1 teaspoon baking soda
- 1 teaspoon grated lemon zest
- 2 cups finely shredded carrots
- ½ cup seedless raisins
- ½ cup chopped walnuts

Icing:

- 8 ounces nonfat or reduced-fat cream cheese
- ¾ cup confectioners' sugar
- 2 teaspoons fresh lemon juice or pure vanilla extract

1. Heat oven to 350°F. Coat two 8-inch round cake pans with nonstick cooking spray and lightly flour them. Mix brown sugar, applesauce, buttermilk, honey, and eggs and white in large bowl; beat until light.

2. In medium-sized bowl, sift flour, cinnamon, salt (if desired), and baking soda. Add gradually to egg mixture. Stir in lemon zest, grated carrots, raisins, and chopped walnuts; pour mixture into pans.

3. Bake until cake begins to separate from sides and center springs back when lightly pressed, about 40 minutes. Cool in pans on rack about 10 minutes. Remove and cool completely on rack.

4. To make icing: Combine all ingredients in food processor bowl; process until smooth. Or mix by hand. When layers are cooled, spread frosting between layers and on top.

Many people mistakenly think that carrot cake is naturally healthful; they couldn't be farther from the truth. These cakes are traditionally made with a load of oil to ensure the moist texture. This truly healthful version replaces the oil with applesauce and the results are amazing.

PER SERVING

CALORIES: **336**
PROTEIN: **9 grams**
FAT: **4 grams**
SODIUM: **263 milligrams**
CHOLESTEROL: **39 milligrams**

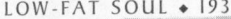

Pineapple Upside-down Cake

The cast-iron skillet classic goes light. For a peachy version, substitute 1 (16-ounce) can peach halves or slices for the pineapple.

◆ 8 SERVINGS

1½ cups cake flour
 2 teaspoons baking powder
½ teaspoon salt (optional)
½ cup butter or margarine, softened
¾ cup granulated sugar
 2 large eggs, separated
½ cup skim or 1-percent-fat milk
 1 teaspoon pure vanilla extract
⅔ cup firmly packed light brown sugar
20-ounce can sliced pineapple, packed in juice, well drained
Optional garnishes: maraschino or pitted fresh cherries,
    Whipped Dessert Topping (page 204)

1. In 8-inch cast-iron skillet over medium heat, melt 2 tablespoons butter. Sprinkle evenly with brown sugar; arrange 7 pineapple slices over brown sugar in single layer. Cut remaining 3 slices pineapple into halves; stand each half slice cut-edge up around inside of skillet.

2. Heat oven to 350°F. In medium-sized bowl, combine cake flour, baking powder, and (if desired) salt. In large mixer bowl, cream remaining 6 tablespoons butter or margarine with granulated sugar until light and fluffy. Add egg yolks one at a time, beating well after each addition.

3. Stir flour mixture into creamed mixture alternately with milk, beginning and ending with flour. In small deep bowl, beat egg whites until stiff peaks form; fold into batter until smooth. Stir in vanilla. Pour batter carefully and evenly over pineapple. Bake until toothpick inserted in center comes out clean, about 40 to 45 minutes. Run small knife around inside edge of pan; invert onto heatproof cake plate; leave skillet over cake a few minutes, then remove. Garnish with cherries and dollops of topping if you like.

Decadent Devil's Food Cake with Creamy Fudge Frosting

◆ 20 SERVINGS

½ teaspoon margarine (for greasing pan)
2 cups unbleached all-purpose flour
1¾ cups sugar
½ cup unsweetened cocoa powder
1 tablespoon baking soda
⅔ cup vegetable oil
1 cup low-fat buttermilk
1 cup strong coffee (instant coffee is fine)

Creamy Fudge Frosting:

◆ ENOUGH TO FROST A 9-BY-13-INCH CAKE, ONE
8-INCH LAYER CAKE, OR ABOUT 20 CUPCAKES

5 tablespoons nonfat cream cheese
1 tablespoon plus 1 teaspoon skim milk
1 teaspoon pure vanilla extract
2 tablespoons unsweetened cocoa powder
3 cups sifted confectioners' sugar

1. Heat oven to 350°F. With margarine, grease and flour 9-by-13-inch baking pan; set aside. Into large mixing bowl, sift together flour, sugar, cocoa, and baking soda. Add vegetable oil and buttermilk. Stir until well blended. Set aside.

2. In small saucepan over medium-high heat, bring coffee to boil; remove from heat. Stir coffee gently into batter. Mixture will be soupy. Pour batter into prepared pan; bake 35 to 40 minutes. Remove from oven and serve warm and plain, or let cool to room temperature.

Coffee mingles with cocoa to give this sinfully delicious cake its rich taste and deep color. It makes enough to serve 20—perfect for your next gathering or to take to a potluck supper. Several years ago I borrowed this recipe from the AMERICAN HEART ASSOCIATION Cookbook, 5th Edition, but I've used it so often, it now seems like mine. It's yours now; take credit!

PER SERVING PLAIN

CALORIES: 253
PROTEIN: 3 grams
FAT: 8 grams
SODIUM: 227 milligrams
CHOLESTEROL: 1 milligram

FROSTING PER SERVING

CALORIES: 63
PROTEIN: 1 gram
FAT: 0 grams
SODIUM: 22 milligrams
CHOLESTEROL: 1 milligram

3. Meanwhile, make frosting: In large mixing bowl, blend cream cheese, I tablespoon milk, and vanilla. Stir in cocoa, blending well. Add remaining I teaspoon milk and ½ cup confectioners' sugar, beating constantly. Half cup at a time, add remaining sugar. Spread frosting on completely cooled cake.

Grandma's Gingerbread with Lemon Sauce

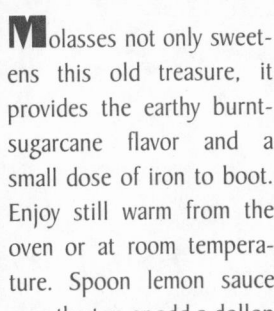

◆ 9 TO 12 SERVINGS

Nonstick cooking spray
½ cup vegetable oil
1 large egg, beaten
⅓ cup packed brown sugar
2½ cups unbleached all-purpose flour
1 teaspoon baking powder
1 teaspoon baking soda
2 teaspoons ground ginger
1 teaspoon ground cinnamon
½ teaspoon salt (optional)
1 cup frozen apple juice concentrate, thawed, or water
1 cup dark unsulfured molasses
½ cup raisins

Lemon Sauce:

◆ 1 CUP

⅓ cup fresh lemon juice
½ cup sugar
1 tablespoon cornstarch
¼ cup water
2 teaspoons butter

Molasses not only sweetens this old treasure, it provides the earthy burnt-sugarcane flavor and a small dose of iron to boot. Enjoy still warm from the oven or at room temperature. Spoon lemon sauce over the top or add a dollop of whipped topping.

PER EACH OF 12 PLAIN SERVINGS

CALORIES: **326**
PROTEIN: **4 grams**
FAT: **10 grams**
SODIUM: **176 milligrams**
CHOLESTEROL: **18 milligrams**

LEMON SAUCE PER SERVING

CALORIES: **42**
PROTEIN: **0 grams**
FAT: **1 gram**
SODIUM: **7 milligrams**
CHOLESTEROL: **2 milligrams**

1. Preheat oven to 350°F. Coat 8-inch-square baking pan with nonstick cooking spray; set aside. In large bowl, combine vegetable oil, egg, and brown sugar; beat until light and fluffy.

2. In large bowl, combine flour, baking powder, baking soda, spices, and (if desired) salt; mix well.

3. In small saucepan, heat apple juice concentrate (or water) to boiling; stir in molasses until blended. Alternately add

dry ingredients and molasses mixture to sugar mixture until blended. Stir in raisins.

4. Pour batter into prepared pan; bake until wooden pick inserted in center comes out almost clean (a crumb or two is okay), about 40 minutes. Cool cake in pan for 10 minutes; run knife or metal spatula around edges to loosen. Turn out onto cake rack and cool completely or serve warm. Cut into squares or rectangles; spoon lemon sauce on top, if you like.

5. To make lemon sauce: Combine lemon juice and sugar in small saucepan. Heat over low heat until sugar is dissolved. In small bowl blend cornstarch and water; pour into sweetened lemon juice. Cook, stirring constantly, just until thickened, about 1 to 2 minutes. Remove from heat; stir in butter. Serve warm or chilled. This sauce also goes well over rice pudding, angel food cake, mixed fresh fruit cups, or vanilla ice cream.

Bread Pudding with Tipsy Raisin Sauce

◆ 8 SERVINGS

Nonstick cooking spray
 1 egg
 2 egg whites
 2 cups skim milk
 ¼ cup granulated sugar
 ¼ cup packed brown sugar
 1 teaspoon pure vanilla extract
 1 teaspoon grated lemon zest
 ½ teaspoon ground cinnamon
 ¼ teaspoon ground nutmeg
 ⅛ teaspoon ground cloves
 1-pound loaf stale French bread, cut or torn into 1-inch
     pieces or 8 slices stale whole wheat bread

Tipsy Raisin Sauce:

◆ ABOUT 1 CUP

 ½ cup raisins
 ¼ cup dark rum
 ¼ cup sugar
 ¼ cup water
 ¼ cup orange juice
 1 tablespoon butter
 2 teaspoons cornstarch

No matter what the season, this ingenious use of stale bread, devised by Creole cooks, can bring pleasure to your table. Embellish the basic recipe with the raisin sauce or with flaked coconut, toasted nuts, crushed pineapple, shredded apple, or even cocoa powder.

PER PLAIN SERVING

CALORIES: **153**
PROTEIN: **6 grams**
FAT: **2 grams**
SODIUM: **188 milligrams**
CHOLESTEROL: **28 milligrams**

TIPSY RAISIN SAUCE PER 2-TABLESPOON SERVING

CALORIES: **86**
PROTEIN: **0 grams**
FAT: **1 gram**
SODIUM: **16 milligrams**
CHOLESTEROL: **4 milligrams**

1. Heat oven to 350°F. Coat 1½-quart baking dish with nonstick cooking spray; set aside. In large bowl, beat egg, egg whites, and milk. Stir in granulated and brown sugar, vanilla, lemon zest, and spices; blend well. Stir in bread cubes; let rest about 10 minutes.

2. Pour bread mixture into prepared baking dish. Set dish in baking pan; place on oven rack. Fill pan halfway up side of casserole with boiling water. Bake until knife inserted in

center of pudding comes out clean, about 1 hour. Let sit for at least 10 minutes before serving. Serve warm or at room temperature. Refrigerate any leftovers.

3. To make sauce: In small bowl, combine raisins and rum; let raisins plump about 20 minutes. In small saucepan over medium heat, combine sugar and water; cook and stir until mixture boils. Cook about 5 minutes longer; remove from heat. Stir in raisin mixture, orange juice, butter, and cornstarch.

4. Return to heat; cook and stir just until mixture thickens. Let cool until warm. This all-purpose dessert sauce adds more yum to bread pudding, rice pudding, sweet potato pie, apple pie, and ice cream. Be sure to keep portions small when adding a topping—the interplay of exciting flavors makes a little go a long way.

Creamy Rice Pudding with Dried Fruit and Nutmeg

◆ 6 SERVINGS

Nonstick cooking spray

 1 large egg

⅓ cup granulated sugar

 2 cups cooked rice

 2 cups evaporated skimmed milk

 1 teaspoon freshly grated nutmeg

½ teaspoon pure vanilla extract

½ cup chopped dried apricots, peaches, pineapple, or other dried fruit, soaked and drained

½ cup chopped dried dates

Optional garnishes: toasted slivered almonds or chopped pecans

1. Heat oven to 350°F. Lightly coat 1½-quart baking dish with nonstick cooking spray; set aside. In mixing bowl, beat egg and sugar and stir in rice. Pour in milk, nutmeg, and vanilla, mixing well. Stir in fruit.

2. Pour into prepared baking dish. Place baking dish into deep baking pan large enough for dish to sit flat on bottom. Fill pan with boiling water halfway up sides of baking dish. Bake, uncovered, stirring once or twice, until knife inserted halfway between center and edge comes out clean, about 50 minutes. Sprinkle with nuts, if desired; serve warm.

Recycling never tasted so good. This dreamy pudding is an ideal way to use leftover rice. An accommodating dish, rice pudding allows you to add any number of interesting ingredients.

PER SERVING

CALORIES: **259**

PROTEIN: **10 grams**

FAT: **1 gram**

SODIUM: **111 milligrams**

CHOLESTEROL: **38 milligrams**

Indian Pudding

This soft-textured, caramel-flavored dessert celebrates the Native Americans' gift of maize. Though the ingredients are easy to assemble, a great deal of patience is required during the long, slow baking, as the tempting aromas fill the kitchen.

◆ 6 SERVINGS

⅔ cup yellow cornmeal
1 quart milk
½ cup dark unsulfured molasses
¼ cup packed brown sugar
1 tablespoon butter or margarine
1 teaspoon grated lemon zest
½ teaspoon ground cinnamon
½ teaspoon ground ginger
½ cup seedless raisins (optional)
1 large egg, slightly beaten
Optional garnish: Whipped Dessert Topping (page 204) or
    low-fat vanilla ice cream sprinkled with ground nutmeg

1. Heat oven to 300°F. In small bowl, mix cornmeal and 1 cup milk. Heat remaining 3 cups milk in top of double boiler over simmering water until steaming. Mix in cornmeal mixture; cook 15 to 20 minutes, stirring occasionally. Stir in molasses and brown sugar; cook 2 to 3 minutes.

2. Remove from heat. Stir in butter, lemon zest, spices, and, if desired, raisins. In small bowl, temper egg by slowly stirring in small amounts of milk mixture until fully blended, not letting eggs scramble.

3. Pour egg mixture back into double boiler, stirring slowly. Into 2-quart casserole sprayed with nonstick cooking spray, spoon pudding mixture. Bake, uncovered, until table knife inserted midway between center and rim comes out clean, about 2 hours. Serve warm with dessert topping or vanilla ice cream dusted with nutmeg.

Coral Reef Mango Sorbet

◆ 6 SERVINGS

3 large ripe mangoes
¼ cup granulated sugar
2 tablespoons fresh lemon juice
Optional garnishes: fresh berries, mint sprigs

1. With sharp knife, carefully peel skin from mangoes. Cut flesh into lengthwise slices; discard seed. Chop flesh to make about 3 cups. In covered blender or food processor container at low speed, blend mangoes, sugar, and lemon juice until mixture is smooth.

2. Pour into 8-inch-square baking pan; cover with foil or plastic wrap. Place in freezer until partially frozen, about 2 hours. Spoon mango mixture into chilled large bowl. With mixer at high speed, beat until fluffy.

3. Return mixture to baking pan; freeze until firm, about 1 hour. To serve, remove mango sorbet from freezer. For easier scooping, let stand at room temperature 10 minutes. Scoop sorbet into serving dish or bowls. Garnish with berries and mint, if desired.

Find a good fruit market where a variety of tropical fruits can be discovered and sampled. The remarkable flavor and color of ripe mangoes make this no-fat sorbet a perfect, refreshing summertime dessert. For an elegant luncheon or dinner party, serve this frozen confection as a palate cleanser between courses, or as a final flourish with Fat-Free Angel Food Cake (page 191) and/or Tropical Ambrosia (page 182).

PER SERVING

CALORIES: **135**
PROTEIN: **1 gram**
FAT: **0 grams**
SODIUM: **3 milligrams**
CHOLESTEROL: **0 milligrams**

Whipped Dessert Topping

Zero grams of fat! Recklessly add a thick dollop to servings of cake, pie, pudding, or fruit.

◆ 4½ CUPS; 18 SERVINGS

 1 cup evaporated skim milk
¼ to ½ cup confectioners' (powdered) sugar
 1 tablespoon fresh lemon juice
½ teaspoon pure vanilla extract or almond extract

1. Pour evaporated milk into small mixer bowl. Chill with beaters in freezer about 30 minutes or until ice crystals form around edge of bowl.

2. Beat on high speed for 1 minute or until very frothy. Gradually add sugar, lemon juice, and vanilla. Continue beating until mixture is stiff, about 2 additional minutes. Serve immediately. Makes 4½ cups.

Index

All-purpose vegetable broth, 18
Angel food cake, 191–92
Apples(s):
    baked, maple, 190
    pancakes, 175
    and walnut muffins, 173
Applesauce, as fat substitute, 180
Aroma-enhancing ingredients, 6–7
Aunt Bertha's corn pudding, 44

Bacon-flavored bits, 33
Baked apples, maple, 190
Bamboo steamer baskets, 84
Banana(s):
    cream pie, 187
    mashed, as fat substitute, 180
    pancakes, 175
Barbecued:
    beef brisket, 141
    beef sandwiches, 150
    Cornish game hens, peachy, 119–20
    short ribs, 142
Basil leaves, 33
Basmati rice, 64
Bayou dirty rice, 72
Bean(s):
    black (SEE Black beans)
    black-eyed peas (SEE Black-eyed peas)
    butter, soup, 30
    field peas, fresh, with whole okra, 55
    succotash, southern-style, 43
    and vegetable chili, fireball, 56–57
    and vegetable stew, Moroccan-style, 54

Beef:
    bell peppers, overstuffed, 148
    brisket, Texas barbecued, 141
    and broccoli stir-fry, gingery, 146–47
    cubed steaks with Creole sauce, 143
    cuts of, 138
    ground, 138
    and macaroni skillet, 149
    pepper steak, savory, 144–45
    pot roast, wine-braised, 140
    sandwiches, barbecued, 150
    short ribs, barbecued, 142
Bell peppers:
    for extra taste and color appeal, 38–39
    green, 6
    overstuffed, 148
Beta carotene, 4
"Big Easy" shrimp Creole, 96
Biscuits:
    baking tips, 166
    buttermilk, basic, 167
    quick drop, 168
    whole wheat, 169
Bisque, shrimp, 25
Black bean(s):
    with marinated tomatoes, Brazilian-style, 58
    and smoked chicken salad, 126
    soup with coriander cream, Cuban-style, 28–29
Black-eyed pea(s), 4
    hip hoppin John, 71
    salad with lemon vinaigrette, 59
Blue crab cakes with fresh corn relish, 99–100
Bountiful vegetable soup, 31
Bouquet garni, 39

Monkfish, 83–84
Monosaturated fats, 8, 9
Moroccan-style vegetable stew, 54
Muffin cups, 157
Muffins:
    apple-walnut, 173
    corn, honey-pecan, 172
    sweet potato, 171
Mushrooms, as soup garnish, 33
Mussels, 83–84

Nonstick vegetable cooking spray, 9,
    139
Noodles, peanutty, 78
Nutritional analysis, 9–11
Nut(s):
    pancakes, 175
    (SEE ALSO names of nuts)

Oatmeal-raisin bread, 170
Oils:
    salad, reversing ratio of vinegar to, 39
    (SEE ALSO Cooking oils; names of oils)
Okra, 5
    in gumbo, 20, 21
    oven "fried," 51
    preparation of, 55
    whole, with fresh field peas, 55
Old-fashioned:
    chicken and dumpling's, 115–16
    chicken soup, 20
Old-time hoecakes, 163
Olive oil, 8, 9, 157
Olivier's, 21
Omega-3 fatty acids, 24, 83
Onions, 6
Orange:
    sweet potato soufflé, 46
    and vanilla french toast, 176
Orange roughy, 83–84
Oven frying, 85
Overcooking, 13
Overstuffed bell peppers, 148
Overweight, 12
Oyster(s):
    dressing, 165
    scalloped, 95

Paella, 97–98
Palm kernel oil, 9
Palm oil, 9
Pancakes, light-as-a-feather, 175
Pans, for baking breads, 156
Paprika, 33
Parmesan cheese, 33
Parsley, 13
Party time curried chicken sandwiches, 127
Pasta:
    chicken spaghetti, 117
    macaroni (SEE Macoroni)
    peanutty noodles, 78
    seafood lasagna, 101–102
Peach:
    fresh, cobbler, 184–85
    preserves barbecue sauce, Cornish hens in,
        119–20
Peanut butter with noodles, 78
Peanut oil, 8, 9
Peanut(s), 27
    with rice and chicken salad, 73
    soup, southern, 27
Pea(s):
    black-eyed (SEE Black-eyed peas)
    field, fresh, with whole okra, 55
Pecan-honey corn muffins, 172
Peppers (SEE Bell peppers; Chili peppers)
Pepper steak, savory, 144–45
Picnic potato salad, 52
Pie:
    banana cream, 187
    lemon icebox, in almond crust, 186
    open-face, 180
    sweet potato, 188
Piecrust, basic, 189
Pilaf with coconut, Caribbean-style, 69
Pineapple:
    and honey glazed yams, 47
    upside-down cake, 194
Polyunsaturated fats, 8, 9, 24
Pork:
    cuts of, 138
    sausage (SEE Sausage)
Potato(es):
    mashed, with garlic, 50
    and rutabagas, mashed, 49

Texas barbecued beef brisket, 141
Tiliapa, 84
Tomato(es):
    marinated, with black beans, Brazilian-style, 58
    as soup garnish, 33
    sun-dried, with collard greens, 40
Topping, whipped, 204
Tortilla chips, as soup garnish, 33
Trans-fatty acids, 8, 9
Tropical ambrosia, 182
Tropical oils, 9
Trout, brook, golden grilled stuffed, 93
Tub (reduced-fat) margarine, 9
Tuna:
    canned, 84
    casserole, 105
Turkey:
    bacon and ham, 139
    carcass, for soup flavoring, 17
    chili for a crowd, 131–32
    fat reduction tips, 108–109
    ground, 107
    meatloaf, savory, 128
    substituting for red meats, 13
    tamale pie, 129–30
Turnip tops and bottoms, 53

"Up north" corn bread, 159
Upside-down cake, pineapple, 194

Vanilla-orange french toast, 176
Vegetable juices, cooking rice with, 64
Vegetable oils (SEE Cooking oils; Salad oils)
Vegetable(s), 37–54
    broth, all-purpose, 18
    and chicken, curried, 114

chili, fireball, 56–57
extending meats with, 139
and eye appeal, 13, 38–39
fat reduction tips, 38
-meat ratio, 13
precooking, for soup, 17
soup, 31
starchy, for soup "creaminess," 17
stew, Moroccan-style, 54
(SEE ALSO specific vegetables)
Vinegars, 7, 39

Walnut-apple muffins, 173
Watermelon(s), 5
    bowl, fruit salad in, 183
Weekday beef and macaroni skillet, 149
Whipped:
    dessert topping, 204
    margarine (low-fat), 9
Whole wheat:
    biscuits, 169
    flour, 156
    pancakes, 175
Wine:
    as flavoring, 7
    Mahimahi marinated with, 92
    pot roast braised with, 140
Wishbone, 109

Yams, honey-pineapple glazed, 47
Yogurt:
    as fat substitute, 180
    reduced-fat or low-fat, 180
Yukon potatoes, 50

Zests, 6

Judd Pilossof

About the Author

JONELL NASH is the acclaimed food editor of ESSENCE magazine. She is the author of a previous cookbook, ESSENCE BRINGS YOU GREAT COOKING. A graduate of Wayne State University, Jonell Nash cooks in an apartment in New York City and a farmhouse in Connecticut.